GROKKING
— THE —
SQL INTERVIEW

JAVINPAUL @JAVINPAUL

Grokking the SQL Interview

© 2023, Javin Paul

Version 1.0 - August 2023

Table of Content

Overview

As a Java developer who has cleared SQL interviews, I can attest that SQL interviews are not easy, given the vast nature of SQL and the variety of concepts and topics it covers. When I was preparing for Java interviews, I was looking for a resource where I learn and prepare SQL questions from a programmer's perspective rather than a DBA, but I couldn't find any. Grokking the SQL Interview is my effort to fill that gap and become an excellent resource for anyone looking to master SQL and prepare for SQL interviews.

Whenever I prepare for Java Interview, I always prepare about SQL and Linux; these are everywhere. That's why I decided to cover essential topics from an interview perspective when I thought to write about this book.

The book covers a wide range of topics, starting with the basics of SQL and database design, and progressing to more advanced topics like SQL queries, joins, indexes, group-by and aggregate functions, stored procedures, triggers and views, database normalization, transactions, window functions, and common interview questions.

One of the best things about this book is that it includes many real-world SQL questions commonly asked in job interviews. This means that by studying the questions and answers in this book, you will be well-prepared for any SQL interview.

Overall, I hope Grokking the SQL Interview is an excellent resource for anyone looking to master SQL and prepare for SQL interviews. I have tried my best to cover all the essential topics you need to know to succeed in SQL interviews. Whether you are a beginner or an experienced SQL developer, you can use this book to quickly revise and prepare for SQL questions for software developer and Data Science interviews.

Why Prepare for SQL and Database for Interviews?

Many Java developers, particularly experienced developers with a couple of years of experience, think that it's not necessary to prepare for SQL questions, only to fluff their chances. It doesn't matter how many years of experience you have in SQL and Database; you must prepare for interviews.

Why? I suggest preparing because when you work on a vast technology like Database and SQL, you work on a particular area. It's almost impossible to learn all the areas of a specific framework.

For example, if you work in a Java application that uses MySQL on the backend, you are most likely exposed to writing queries and stored procedures. Still, you may or may not be involved in the database design process.

And, believe it or not, interviews are almost always very different from real jobs. Interviewers expect you to know everything about the technology, even if certain areas are never used in any project, like normalization and database design in this case.

If your aim is to clear the interviews because you need that job then you don't have any choice; you cannot argue what is right or what is wrong, the best approach is to prepare hard and prepare well and that's where this book can help you.

While learning anything quickly is impossible, this book provides a nice overview of almost all essential SQL and Database concepts. You can easily finish the book in a few hours or few days, depending on how much time you spend daily.

If you are going for a Software Developer interview or Data Science Interview, where SQL and Database is mentioned as a desired skill then I highly recommend you to go through these questions before attending any telephonic or face-to-face interview.

While there is no guarantee that the Interviewer will ask any question from this book, by going through the book, you already know most of the SQL and Database concepts which you are expected to know.

How to prepare SQL for Interviews?

In order to best prepare for Software Engineer and Data Science SQL Interviews, you need to have a solid understanding of SQL concepts and their a couple of popular databases like MySQL, Oracle, Microsfot SQL Server, and PostgreSQL

Preparing for SQL interviews requires a combination of theoretical knowledge and practical experience.

Here are some tips to help you prepare for SQL interviews:

- **Review SQL basics:** Ensure you have a solid understanding of SQL fundamentals, including data types, operators, and syntax.

- **Practice SQL queries:** Work on creating and executing SQL queries involving filtering, sorting, grouping, and joining data from multiple tables.

- **Familiarize yourself with popular database management systems:** Get familiar with popular database management systems such as MySQL, Oracle, and SQL Server.

- **Learn about database normalization:** nderstand the basic principles of database normalization, which is organizing data to minimize redundancy.

- **Understand data modeling:** Learn about data modeling, which involves creating a conceptual model of the data to be stored in a database.

- **Brush up on statistics and data analysis:** Many SQL interviews will involve statistical and data analysis questions, so it's important to understand these topics well.

- **Practice with sample SQL interview questions:** There are many resources available online where you can find sample SQL interview questions to practice with.

Remember that SQL interviews are not just about memorizing syntax and queries but also about being able to think critically and solve complex problems. With practice and preparation, you can develop the skills needed to ace your SQL interview. If you are short of time, then there is no choice but to go through the question as soon as possible so that you can revise the essential concepts and at least have some idea about it.

Reviewing this book will not only help you gain both confidence and knowledge to answer the questions, but more importantly, it will allow you to drive the Java interview in your favor. This is the single most important tip I can give you as a Java developer.

Always remember your answers drive interviews, and these questions will empower you to drive the Interviewer to your stronger areas.

All the best for the SQL interview, and if you have any questions or feedback, you can always contact me on Twitter at javinpaul or comment on my blogs **Javarevisited**and **Java67**.

Which SQL and Database topics to Prepare for Interviews?

These are the key SQL and database topics which you need to prepare for any technical interviews:

- SQL and Database Basics
- SQL JOINs
- SQL Queries from Interviews

- Indexes
- GROUP BY
- Aggregate Functions
- Stored Procedure
- Trigger and View
- Advanced SQL Questions
- Conclusion

These are also the topics which you need to prepare Data Scientist interviews, which means you can kill two birds in one stone. I mean, by preparing for Software development interview you can also get yourself ready for potential Data Scientist jobs.

CHAPTER 1

SQL and Database Telephonic Interview Questions

Database and SQL is a very important skill, not just for DBA or Database admins but also for any application developer like <u>Java</u>, <u>.NET</u>, or <u>Web developers</u>. This is why you would often see questions from SQL and Database in Programming interviews.

For DBAs, SQL is more important than a programmer because it being their primary skill, they are also expected to know more than a common Java or .NET developer. Since no Java interview is just about Java questions, I often receive requests from my reader about SQL questions like how to solve a particular query or some tricky questions based upon database indexes.

We will kick start our journey with common SQL questions. So, these are 50 standard SQL and Database interview questions often asked in the telephonic round of DBA and Programmer interviews. Phone interviews differ slightly from face-to-face interviews and tend to be more specific.

Since this is usually a screening round to weed out unsuitable candidates, the interviewer often likes to cover as many concepts as possible. That's why it becomes a test of general knowledge of the developer about a particular skill than the depth of his knowledge.

As I mentioned, on phone interviews, Interviewers are usually in a hurry; they want to hear the correct and concise answer, and not blah blah blah answers; because of that, I have kept answers short and sweet. One more reason for keeping your answer short and specific is to avoid getting shot by providing additional information which is not accurate.

At the same time, It's also hard for any SQL developer to go through five-page articles to revise some 30 most frequently asked SQL questions, keep answers to the point helps them a lot.

So, let's start our journey with these beautiful databases and SQL interview questions, I am sure you will also learn new things.

Question 1

Difference between UNION and UNION ALL in SQL

Short answer - UNION doesn't include duplicate records, UNION ALL does. Both can be used to combine results from multiple queries.

Long answer - In SQL, both **UNION** and **UNION ALL** are used to combine the results of two or more **SELECT** queries into a single result set. However, there is a significant difference between the two:

1. UNION:

- **UNION** combines the results of multiple **SELECT** queries and removes duplicate rows from the final result set.
- It performs an implicit **DISTINCT** operation on the result set, ensuring that only distinct rows are included.
- It is useful when you want to combine and eliminate duplicate data from multiple tables or queries.

2. UNION ALL:

- **UNION ALL** also combines the results of multiple **SELECT** queries, but it includes all rows, even if there are duplicates.

- It does not perform any duplicate elimination, resulting in faster performance compared to **UNION**, especially when dealing with large datasets.
- It is useful when you want to combine and preserve all rows, including duplicates, from multiple tables or queries.

Example:

Consider two tables, **employees** and **contractors**, with similar structures:

1. employees table:

emp_id	emp_name	emp_salary
1	John	50000
2	Jane	55000
3	Mary	60000
4	Peter	52000

2. contractors table:

contractor_id	contractor_name	contractor_salary
101	Sam	48000
102	Kate	51000
103	Alice	48000
104	Mike	52000

1. Using **UNION**:

```
SELECT emp_id, emp_name, emp_salary FROM employees
UNION
SELECT contractor_id, contractor_name, contractor_salary FROM contractors;
```

emp_id	emp_name	emp_salary
1	John	50000
2	Jane	55000
3	Mary	60000
4	Peter	52000
101	Sam	48000
102	Kate	51000
103	Alice	48000
104	Mike	52000

As you can see, **UNION** combined the data from both tables and removed duplicates (e.g., contractor with salary 48000 is only shown once).

2. Using **UNION ALL**:

```
SELECT emp_id, emp_name, emp_salary FROM employees
UNION ALL
SELECT contractor_id, contractor_name, contractor_salary FROM contractors;
```

Result:

emp_id	emp_name	emp_salary
1	John	50000
2	Jane	55000
3	Mary	60000
4	Peter	52000
101	Sam	48000

102	Kate	51000
103	Alice	48000
104	Mike	52000

In this case, **UNION ALL** also combined the data from both tables but retained duplicates in the result set. As a result, contractor with salary 48000 is shown twice, as there are two contractors with that salary.

Question 2

Difference between WHERE and HAVING clause in SQL?

Short answer - In case of WHERE filtering applies before aggregation while in case of HAVING, filtering applies after aggregation

Long answer - The WHERE and HAVING clauses are both used in SQL to filter data, but they serve different purposes:

1. WHERE Clause:

- The **WHERE** clause is used to filter rows before they are grouped or aggregated in the query.
- It operates on individual rows of the table and filters rows based on specified conditions.
- It is typically used with non-aggregate functions and helps to reduce the number of rows considered for grouping and aggregation.

2. HAVING Clause:

- The **HAVING** clause is used to filter the result of a grouped query, specifically after the **GROUP BY** clause has been applied.
- It operates on groups of rows and filters groups based on specified conditions.

- It is used in combination with aggregate functions (e.g., **COUNT, SUM, AVG**, etc.) and allows you to filter the grouped data based on aggregate results.

Example:

Consider a table named **employees** with the following data:

emp_id	emp_name	department	salary
1	John	HR	50000
2	Jane	IT	55000
3	Mary	HR	60000
4	Peter	IT	52000

1. Using WHERE clause:

Suppose we want to retrieve the employees who belong to the HR department and have a salary greater than 55000:

```
SELECT emp_id, emp_name, department, salary
FROM employees
WHERE department = 'HR' AND salary > 55000;
```

Result:

emp_id	emp_name	department	salary
3	Mary	HR	60000

In this example, the **WHERE** clause filters individual rows of the **employees** table based on the conditions specified (**department = 'HR'** and **salary > 55000**).

2. Using HAVING clause:

Suppose we want to retrieve the departments with an average salary greater than 51000:

```
SELECT department, AVG(salary) AS avg_salary
FROM employees
GROUP BY department
HAVING AVG(salary) > 51000;
```

Result:

department	avg_salary
HR	55000
IT	53500

In this example, the **HAVING** clause operates on the result of the grouped query (after applying **GROUP BY department**) and filters the groups based on the condition specified (**AVG(salary) > 51000**).

In summary, the **WHERE** clause filters individual rows before grouping, while the **HAVING** clause filters groups after grouping has been applied in the query.

Question 3

Describe the difference between clustered and non-clustered indexes in a database?

Short answer - Clustered index defined the order in which data is physically stored in the table. Since data can be sorted in only one way physically, there is only one clustered index per table and that's usually the primary key. You can have multiple non-clustered indexes to speed up your queries.

Long answer - In SQL, both clustered and non-clustered indexes are used to improve the performance of database queries by providing quick access to data. However, there are significant differences between the two:

1. Clustered Index:

- A clustered index determines the physical order of data rows in a table. Each table can have only one clustered index.

- When a table has a clustered index, the rows are stored in the order of the clustered index key. This means that the data is physically organized on disk based on the values in the indexed column.
- Due to the physical ordering, the retrieval of rows using a clustered index is faster when querying on the indexed column.
- Creating or rebuilding a clustered index can be more time-consuming, as it affects the physical order of data in the table.

Example:

Consider a table named **employees** with the following data:

emp_id	emp_name	department	salary
1	John	HR	50000
2	Jane	IT	55000
3	Mary	HR	60000
4	Peter	IT	52000

If we create a clustered index on the **emp_id** column:

```
CREATE CLUSTERED INDEX idx_emp_id ON employees(emp_id);
```

The data in the **employees** table will be physically sorted based on the values in the **emp_id** column. Any query that uses the **emp_id** column as a search criteria will benefit from faster data retrieval.

2. Non-Clustered Index:

- A non-clustered index is a separate data structure that contains a copy of the indexed columns along with a pointer to the actual data rows in the table.

- A table can have multiple non-clustered indexes, allowing for different indexing strategies to optimize various queries.
- Non-clustered indexes do not affect the physical order of data in the table; instead, they provide a quick lookup path to the actual data rows.
- Non-clustered indexes are generally faster to create or rebuild compared to clustered indexes.

Example:

If we create a non-clustered index on the **salary** column:

```
CREATE NONCLUSTERED INDEX idx_salary ON employees(salary);
```

The index will contain a copy of the **salary** column along with pointers to the actual rows in the **employees** table. Any query that uses the **salary** column in a search or join operation will benefit from faster data retrieval.

In summary, a clustered index determines the physical order of data in a table and can only be created on one column, while a non-clustered index is a separate data structure that allows for multiple indexing strategies and does not affect the physical order of data. The choice between a clustered and non-clustered index depends on the specific database design and the types of queries that need optimization.

Question 4

Write an SQL query to find the second highest salary of an employee without using TOP or LIMIT?

You can use correlated queries to solve this problem. You can find the second highest salary of an employee without using TOP or LIMIT by using the following SQL query:

```
SELECT DISTINCT salary
FROM employees
WHERE salary < (
    SELECT MAX(salary) FROM employees
)
ORDER BY salary DESC
LIMIT 1;
```

In this query, we are using a subquery to find the maximum salary in the **employees** table. Then, we are selecting all distinct salary values that are less than the maximum salary. Finally, we order the results in descending order and use **LIMIT 1** to get the second highest salary.

Question 5

How to find duplicate rows in the database?

To find duplicate rows in a database table, you can use SQL queries with the **GROUP BY** and **HAVING** clauses.

The **GROUP BY** clause groups the rows with identical values, and the **HAVING** clause filters the groups to show only those with more than one occurrence. Here's an example of how to find duplicate rows in a table:

Suppose we have a table named **employees** with the following data:

emp_id	emp_name	department	salary
1	John	HR	50000
2	Jane	IT	55000
3	Mary	HR	60000
4	Peter	IT	52000
5	Alice	HR	50000

| 6 | Tom | IT | 52000 |
| 7 | Emma | HR | 60000 |

To find duplicate rows based on the **salary** and **department** columns, you can use the following SQL query:

```
SELECT salary, department, COUNT(*) AS duplicate_count
FROM employees
GROUP BY salary, department
HAVING COUNT(*) > 1;
```

The result of the query will be:

salary	department	duplicate_count
50000	HR	2
60000	HR	2
52000	IT	2

In this example, the query groups the rows based on the **salary** and **department** columns and counts the occurrences of each group. The **HAVING COUNT(*) > 1** condition filters the groups to show only those with more than one occurrence, indicating that these are the duplicate rows in the table.

Please note that the example assumes you are using SQL, and the syntax may vary slightly depending on the database management system you are using (e.g., MySQL, SQL Server, PostgreSQL, etc.). Additionally, the duplicate criteria can be based on different combinations of columns as needed for your specific use case.

Question 6

Difference between correlated and non-correlated subquery in SQL?

In SQL, subqueries are queries that are nested within another query. Subqueries can be classified into two types: correlated subqueries and non-correlated subqueries. The main difference between them lies in how they interact with the outer query:

1. Non-Correlated Subquery:

- A non-correlated subquery is an independent query that can be executed on its own without reference to the outer query.
- The subquery is evaluated first, and its result is then used in the outer query to filter or perform other operations.
- Non-correlated subqueries are executed only once, regardless of the number of rows in the outer query, making them generally more efficient.

Example of a non-correlated subquery:

Consider a table named **employees** with the following data:

emp_id	emp_name	department	salary
1	John	HR	50000
2	Jane	IT	55000
3	Mary	HR	60000
4	Peter	IT	52000

Suppose we want to find all employees whose salary is greater than the average salary of all employees. We can use a non-correlated subquery for this:

```
SELECT emp_id, emp_name, department, salary
FROM employees
WHERE salary > (
    SELECT AVG(salary)
    FROM employees
);
```

In this example, the subquery **(SELECT AVG(salary) FROM employees)** is evaluated only once and provides the average salary value. The outer query then uses this value to filter the employees whose salary is greater than the average.

2. *Correlated Subquery:*

- A correlated subquery is a subquery that depends on the values from the outer query to execute.
- For each row processed by the outer query, the subquery is re-evaluated with the specific values from the current row of the outer query.
- Correlated subqueries can lead to decreased performance, especially when dealing with large datasets, as they may be executed multiple times.

Example of a correlated subquery:

Suppose we want to find all employees whose salary is greater than the average salary of their respective departments. We can use a correlated subquery for this:

```sql
SELECT emp_id, emp_name, department, salary
FROM employees e1
WHERE salary > (
    SELECT AVG(salary)
    FROM employees e2
    WHERE e1.department = e2.department
);
```

In this example, the subquery **(SELECT AVG(salary) FROM employees e2 WHERE e1.department = e2.department)** is correlated to the outer query by the **department** column. For each row processed by the outer query (e1), the subquery is re-evaluated with the specific department value from the current row of the outer query.

In summary, the main difference between correlated and non-correlated subqueries is that correlated subqueries depend on the values from the outer query and are re-evaluated for each row of the outer query, while non-correlated subqueries are independent and executed only once. Non-correlated subqueries are generally more efficient, but correlated subqueries are necessary when you need to access values from the outer query within the subquery's logic.

Question 7

How many clustered indexes you can have in a table?

Short answer - This is a tricky question, you can only have one clustered index per table.

Long answer - In most relational database management systems (RDBMS), a table can have only one clustered index. The clustered index determines the physical order of data rows in the table, and each table can be physically organized in only one way.

However, it's essential to note that a table can have multiple non-clustered indexes. Non-clustered indexes are separate data structures that provide quick access paths to the data rows in the table. While there can be multiple non-clustered indexes, there can be only one clustered index per table.

The limitation of one clustered index per table is mainly due to the fact that **the physical order of data rows can only be maintained in one specific way**.

Having multiple clustered indexes would require storing the same data in multiple physical orders, which would be inefficient and impractical. Hence, the single clustered index restriction is enforced to maintain data consistency and storage efficiency.

In summary, a table in most RDBMS can have only one clustered index, but it can have multiple non-clustered indexes to optimize query performance for various columns and criteria.

Question 8

Difference between the PRIMARY key and the UNIQUE key constraint in SQL?

In SQL, both the PRIMARY key and the UNIQUE key constraint are used to enforce uniqueness in a table's column(s). However, there are some key differences between them:

1. PRIMARY Key Constraint:

- The PRIMARY key constraint is used to uniquely identify each row in a table. It ensures that the values in the specified column(s) are unique and not NULL.

- Each table can have only one PRIMARY key constraint, and it must be defined when the table is created.

- A PRIMARY key column cannot have duplicate or NULL values.

- The PRIMARY key also creates a clustered index on the specified column(s), which determines the physical order of data in the table for efficient data retrieval.

Example:

```
CREATE TABLE employees (
    emp_id INT PRIMARY KEY,
    emp_name VARCHAR(50),
    department VARCHAR(50)
);
```

In this example, the **emp_id** column is designated as the PRIMARY key, ensuring that each employee's ID is unique and not NULL.

2. UNIQUE Key Constraint:

- The UNIQUE key constraint is used to enforce uniqueness in a column(s) but does not necessarily identify each row uniquely.

- A table can have multiple UNIQUE key constraints, and they can be defined when the table is created or added later.

- A UNIQUE key column can have unique values, but it can allow NULL values (except in the case of a composite UNIQUE key where all columns must be unique and not NULL).

- A UNIQUE key creates a non-clustered index on the specified column(s) to optimize data retrieval.

Example:

```
CREATE TABLE students (
    student_id INT,
    student_name VARCHAR(50),
    email VARCHAR(100) UNIQUE
);
```

In this example, the **email** column has a UNIQUE key constraint, ensuring that each email address is unique in the table, but it can allow NULL values.

In summary, both the PRIMARY key and the UNIQUE key constraint ensure uniqueness in column(s) of a table. The PRIMARY key uniquely identifies each row and creates a clustered index, while the UNIQUE key constraint enforces uniqueness but does not necessarily identify each row uniquely and creates a non-clustered index.

The choice between using a PRIMARY key or a UNIQUE key depends on the specific requirements and data model of the table.

Question 9

Difference between view and materialized view in SQL?

In SQL, both views and materialized views are database objects used to provide a logical representation of data from one or more underlying tables. However, there are significant differences between the two:

1. View:

- A view is a virtual table that does not store data on its own. It is defined by a query that retrieves data from one or more base tables.

- Views are used to simplify complex queries, encapsulate data access logic, and provide a security mechanism by restricting access to specific columns or rows of a table.

- Whenever you query a view, the underlying query is executed, and the data is generated on-the-fly based on the latest data in the base tables. The view's data is always up-to-date with the underlying tables.

- Views are suitable for scenarios where real-time data is needed, and you want to hide the complexity of underlying tables.

Example of creating a view:

```
CREATE VIEW employee_details AS
SELECT emp_id, emp_name, department
FROM employees;
```

In this example, the **employee_details** view provides a simplified representation of the data in the **employees** table, containing only the **emp_id**, **emp_name**, and **department** columns.

2. Materialized View:

- A materialized view is a physical copy of the result set of a query. It stores the data in a separate table and keeps the data updated periodically or on-demand based on a defined refresh schedule.

- Materialized views are used to improve query performance by precomputing and storing the results of complex and resource-intensive queries. They are beneficial for scenarios where you need to access the same query result multiple times or when the underlying data changes infrequently.

- The data in a materialized view is not always up-to-date with the underlying tables; it depends on the last refresh or update time. Therefore, materialized views are suitable for scenarios where near-real-time data is sufficient.

Example of creating a materialized view:

```
CREATE MATERIALIZED VIEW mv_employee_details AS
SELECT emp_id, emp_name, department
FROM employees;
```

In this example, the **mv_employee_details** materialized view stores a physical copy of the **emp_id**, **emp_name**, and **department** columns from the **employees** table. The data in the materialized view must be refreshed periodically to stay up-to-date.

In summary, the key difference between a view and a materialized view is that a view is a virtual table that does not store data, while a materialized view is a physical copy of the query result stored in a separate table. Views provide real-time data, while materialized views offer improved query performance by precomputing and storing query results, but they may have slightly stale data depending on the refresh schedule.

Question 10

Difference between TRUNCATE, DELETE and DROP in SQL?

Delete removes record but also put an entry into log segment so you can roll back, truncate removes all rows of a table without logging each record on log segment, DROP removes table itself.

In SQL, **TRUNCATE**, **DELETE**, and **DROP** are used to remove data or database objects, but they serve different purposes and have different effects:

1. TRUNCATE:

- **TRUNCATE** is used to delete all the rows from a table while keeping the table structure intact.
- It is a data manipulation language (DML) command that is typically faster than the **DELETE** command because it does not log individual row deletions and does not generate as much undo/redo data.
- The **TRUNCATE** command cannot be used on tables with foreign key constraints, and it also cannot be rolled back.
- When you use **TRUNCATE**, the table's identity counter (if any) is reset, and the table becomes empty.

Example of using **TRUNCATE**:

```
TRUNCATE TABLE employees;
```

This command will remove all rows from the **employees** table, but the table structure will remain unchanged.

2. DELETE:

- **DELETE** is used to remove specific rows from a table based on specified conditions.
- It is a DML command that is slower than **TRUNCATE** because it logs individual row deletions, generates undo/redo data, and performs additional checks for constraints and triggers.
- **DELETE** can be used with a **WHERE** clause to specify the conditions for row deletion.
- The **DELETE** command can be rolled back using the **ROLLBACK** statement.

Example of using **DELETE**:

```
DELETE FROM employees WHERE department = 'HR';
```

This command will delete all rows from the **employees** table where the **department** is 'HR'.

3. DROP:

- **DROP** is used to remove database objects such as tables, views, indexes, or stored procedures.
- It is a data definition language (DDL) command that completely removes the object from the database.
- **DROP** cannot be rolled back, and once an object is dropped, it is permanently deleted from the database.
- Be cautious when using **DROP** as it can lead to data loss if not used carefully.

Example of dropping a table:

```
DROP TABLE employees;
```

This command will remove the **employees** table and all its data and structure from the database.

In summary, **TRUNCATE** is used to remove all rows from a table, **DELETE** is used to remove specific rows based on conditions, and **DROP** is used to remove entire database objects. The choice of which command to use depends on the specific requirements and the impact you want to have on the data or database structure.

Question 11

What is Referential Integrity in a relational database?

Short answer - It's a rule which ensures that when a record is deleted from the primary table, all associated records are deleted from the related table. It ensures data integrity.

Long answer - Referential Integrity is a concept in a relational database that ensures the consistency and validity of data relationships between tables. It is based on the idea of maintaining accurate and reliable relationships among related data across different tables. The primary goal of referential integrity is to prevent orphaned or invalid data and maintain the integrity of the data model.

In a relational database, Referential Integrity is typically enforced using Foreign Key constraints. A Foreign Key is a column or set of columns in a table that refers to the Primary Key of another table. It establishes a relationship between the two tables, where the Foreign Key column(s) in one table hold values that match the Primary Key column(s) in the referenced table.

The key aspects of Referential Integrity are as follows:

1. Primary Key - Foreign Key Relationship:

- The Primary Key column(s) in a table serve as the unique identifier for each row in that table.
- The Foreign Key column(s) in another table reference the Primary Key column(s) of the related table.
- This relationship ensures that each value in the Foreign Key column(s) of the referencing table has a corresponding value in the Primary Key column(s) of the referenced table.

2. Maintaining Data Integrity:

- Referential Integrity ensures that data relationships between tables are maintained accurately.
- It prevents the creation of Foreign Key values in the referencing table that do not exist in the Primary Key of the referenced table, thereby avoiding orphaned or invalid data.

3. Enforcing Constraints:

- Foreign Key constraints are used to enforce Referential Integrity rules in the database.

- These constraints can be declarative (defined explicitly) or implicit (created automatically by the database based on the schema).

4. Cascading Actions:

- Referential Integrity constraints can include cascading actions that define how updates or deletions in the referenced table affect the referencing table.

- Common cascading actions include CASCADE (update/delete the referencing rows), SET NULL (set referencing rows to NULL), and RESTRICT (prevent update/delete if referenced rows exist).

By enforcing Referential Integrity, the database ensures that data relationships are reliable and consistent, thereby maintaining data accuracy and validity. It is an essential concept in relational database design and helps prevent data inconsistencies and integrity issues across related tables.

Question 12

What is Normalization?

Short answer - *A way to avoid duplication of data in tables.*

Long answer - Normalization is the process of organizing and structuring a relational database to reduce data redundancy and improve data integrity. It involves dividing a database into multiple related tables and applying specific rules (normal forms) to ensure that each table serves a single purpose and contains non-redundant data. The main goal of normalization is to eliminate data anomalies and ensure that each piece of data is stored in one place only.

There are different levels of normalization known as normal forms, with each successive normal form building upon the previous ones. The most commonly used normal forms are First Normal Form (1NF), Second Normal Form (2NF), Third Normal Form (3NF), BCNF, and so on.

Let's illustrate normalization with an example:

Consider an unnormalized table named **Students** with the following columns:

Student_ID	Student_Name	Course_Code	Course_Name	Instructor	Instructor_Email
101	John	CS101	Intro to CS	Prof. Smith	smith@example.com
101	John	MATH101	Math Basics	Prof. Johnson	johnson@example.com
102	Alice	CS101	Intro to CS	Prof. Smith	smith@example.com
103	Bob	MATH101	Math Basics	Prof. Johnson	johnson@example.com

This table exhibits data redundancy as both **Student_ID** and **Course_Code** are duplicated, leading to potential inconsistencies and anomalies.

Normalization Process:

Step 1: First Normal Form (1NF)

- In 1NF, we ensure that each cell in the table holds only atomic values (single values).
- To achieve 1NF, we can split the original table into two separate tables: **Students** and **Courses**.

Students Table:

Student_ID	Student_Name
101	John
102	Alice
103	Bob

Courses Table:

Course_Code	Course_Name	Instructor	Instructor_Email
CS101	Intro to CS	Prof. Smith	smith@example.com
MATH101	Math Basics	Prof. Johnson	johnson@example.com

Step 2: Second Normal Form (2NF)

- In 2NF, we ensure that each non-key attribute (column) is fully dependent on the entire primary key.
- The **Courses** table already satisfies 2NF since all non-key attributes (**Course_Name, Instructor, Instructor_Email**) are dependent on the whole primary key (**Course_Code**).

Step 3: Third Normal Form (3NF)

- In 3NF, we ensure that there is no transitive dependency between non-key attributes.
- To achieve 3NF, we can further split the **Courses** table into two separate tables: **Courses** and **Instructors**.

Courses Table:

Course_Code	Course_Name	Instructor_Code
CS101	Intro to CS	1
MATH101	Math Basics	2

Instructors Table:

Instructor_Code	Instructor	Instructor_Email
1	Prof. Smith	smith@example.com
2	Prof. Johnson	johnson@example.com

Now, the data is organized into normalized tables, eliminating data redundancy and ensuring data integrity. Each table serves a single purpose, and data is not duplicated across multiple rows. The relational database is now in Third Normal Form (3NF).

Let's further apply normalization to achieve higher normal forms:

Step 4: Boyce-Codd Normal Form (BCNF)

- In BCNF, we ensure that every determinant (candidate key) in a table uniquely determines all non-key attributes.
- In the **Students** table, the **Student_ID** is the primary key, and it uniquely determines the **Student_Name**.
- Since there is only one determinant, the table already satisfies BCNF.

Step 5: Fourth Normal Form (4NF)

- In 4NF, we ensure that there are no multi-valued dependencies within a table.
- In our example, there is no multi-valued dependency within any table, so the database satisfies 4NF.

Step 6: Fifth Normal Form (5NF)

- In 5NF, we address cases where a table has join dependencies between multi-valued dependencies.
- In our example, there are no such cases, so the database satisfies 5NF.

The final normalized database would look like this:

Students Table:

Student_ID	Student_Name
101	John
102	Alice
103	Bob

Courses Table:

Course_Code	Course_Name	Instructor_Code
CS101	Intro to CS	1
MATH101	Math Basics	2

Instructors Table:

Instructor_Code	Instructor	Instructor_Email
1	Prof. Smith	smith@example.com
2	Prof. Johnson	johnson@example.com

By following the normalization process and dividing the data into separate related tables, we have eliminated data redundancy, reduced update anomalies, and ensured data integrity. Each table serves a single purpose, and the relationships between the tables are defined by appropriate foreign key constraints.

Normalization is an essential practice in database design to create well-structured and efficient databases, making it easier to maintain, update, and retrieve data accurately.

Question 13

When a table is said to be in 1NF, 2nd NF, and 3rd NF?

A table is said to be in First Normal Form (1NF), Second Normal Form (2NF), and Third Normal Form (3NF) based on specific criteria related to data organization and dependencies. Each normal form builds upon the previous one, and a higher normal form indicates a higher level of data integrity and a reduction in data redundancy and anomalies. Here's an overview of each normal form:

1. First Normal Form (1NF):

- A table is in 1NF if it satisfies the following conditions:
  - Each column in the table holds atomic (single) values, meaning no column contains multiple values or sets.
  - Each cell in the table contains a single value (no repeating groups or arrays).

2. Second Normal Form (2NF):

- A table is in 2NF if it satisfies the conditions of 1NF and meets an additional criterion:

o It should have a composite primary key (composed of two or more columns).

o All non-key attributes (columns) in the table should be fully dependent on the entire primary key, not just on part of it.

3. Third Normal Form (3NF):

- A table is in 3NF if it satisfies the conditions of 1NF and 2NF and meets one more criterion:

o It should have no transitive dependencies.

o Transitive dependencies occur when a non-key attribute depends on another non-key attribute rather than directly on the primary key.

In summary, a table is in 1NF if it has atomic values and no repeating groups, 2NF if it has a composite primary key and all non-key attributes depend on the entire primary key, and 3NF if it has no transitive dependencies.

Achieving higher normal forms ensures better data organization, reduces data redundancy, and helps maintain data integrity in a relational database.

It is considered good practice to normalize a database to at least the Third Normal Form to avoid data anomalies and ensure efficient data management.

Question 14

Describe the difference between ISNULL() and COALESCE() in SQL Server?

Both **ISNULL()** and **COALESCE()** are used in SQL Server to handle NULL values, but they have some differences in functionality:

1. ISNULL() Function:

- **ISNULL()** is a built-in SQL Server function that returns the specified replacement value if the expression evaluates to NULL. Otherwise, it returns the original expression.
- It takes two arguments: the expression to be evaluated and the replacement value.
- **ISNULL()** is specific to SQL Server and can only handle two arguments.

Example using **ISNULL()**:

```
SELECT ISNULL(column_name, 'Not available') AS result
FROM table_name;
```

In this example, if **column_name** is NULL, the result will be 'Not available'; otherwise, the result will be the value of **column_name**.

2. COALESCE() Function:

- **COALESCE()** is a standard SQL function supported by various database management systems, including SQL Server.
- It takes multiple arguments and returns the first non-NULL expression from the list. If all arguments are NULL, it returns NULL.
- Unlike **ISNULL()**, **COALESCE()** can handle multiple arguments and will evaluate and return the first non-NULL value encountered.

Example using **COALESCE()**:

```
SELECT COALESCE(column1, column2, column3, 'Not available') AS result
FROM table_name;
```

In this example, **COALESCE()** will return the first non-NULL value among **column1**, **column2**, and **column3**. If all three columns are NULL, it will return 'Not available'.

Key Differences:

- **ISNULL()** takes two arguments, while **COALESCE()** can take multiple arguments.
- **ISNULL()** returns the replacement value if the expression is NULL; **COALESCE()** returns the first non-NULL value from the list of expressions.
- **ISNULL()** is specific to SQL Server, while **COALESCE()** is a standard SQL function supported by many database systems.

In SQL Server, both functions can be useful for handling NULL values, but **COALESCE()** offers more flexibility when dealing with multiple expressions and provides a standard approach that can be easily ported to other SQL-compliant databases.

Question 15

How do you ensure that only values between 1 to 5 are allowed in an integer column?

To ensure that only values between 1 to 5 are allowed in an integer column, you can use a combination of CHECK constraint and a BETWEEN clause. The **CHECK constraint** allows you to define a condition that must be true for any data to be inserted or updated in the column. In this case, you can use the CHECK constraint to enforce the range of values.

Here's an example of how to create a table with an integer column that allows only values between 1 to 5:

```sql
CREATE TABLE your_table (
    your_column INT CHECK (your_column BETWEEN 1 AND 5)
);
```

In this example, the **your_table** has an integer column named **your_column**, and the CHECK constraint ensures that only values between 1 and 5 (inclusive) are allowed in this column. Any attempt to insert or update a value outside this range will result in a constraint violation error, and the operation will be rejected.

Let's demonstrate how you can insert valid and invalid values:

Valid Insert:

```
INSERT INTO your_table (your_column) VALUES (3);
-- This will insert the value 3 into the your_column successfully.
```

Invalid Insert:

```
INSERT INTO your_table (your_column) VALUES (6);
-- This will result in a constraint violation error as 6 is outside the all
```

By using the CHECK constraint with the BETWEEN clause, you can ensure that only valid values are allowed in the integer column, maintaining data integrity and preventing incorrect data from being entered into the table.

Question 16

Difference between CHAR and VARCHAR data types in SQL?

Short answer - CHAR is fixed length, VARCHAR is variable length

Long answer - In SQL, CHAR and VARCHAR are both data types used to store character strings, but they have some key differences in terms of storage and behavior:

1. CHAR Data Type:

- **CHAR** stands for "character" and is used to store fixed-length strings.
- When you define a column with the **CHAR** data type, you need to specify a fixed length for the string, and all values stored in that column will be padded with spaces to fill the entire defined length.
- The storage space for **CHAR** columns is fixed and does not vary based on the actual length of the string. This means

that if you define a **CHAR(10)** column and store a 5-character string in it, it will still occupy 10 characters of storage (5 characters plus 5 spaces).

- Due to the fixed-length nature of **CHAR**, it is more suitable for storing values with a consistent length.

<u>Example of **CHAR**</u>:

```
CREATE TABLE employees (
    emp_id INT,
    emp_name CHAR(20),
    department CHAR(10)
);
```

2. VARCHAR Data Type:

- **VARCHAR** stands for "variable-length character" and is used to store strings of varying lengths.

- Unlike **CHAR**, **VARCHAR** does not pad values with extra spaces and only uses the required amount of storage for each string.

- When you define a column with the **VARCHAR** data type, you need to specify a maximum length for the string, but the actual storage space used will depend on the length of the data stored.

- The storage space for **VARCHAR** columns is more efficient for variable-length data, as it avoids wasting space on padding.

<u>Example of **VARCHAR**</u>:

```
CREATE TABLE employees (
    emp_id INT,
    emp_name VARCHAR(50),
    department VARCHAR(30)
);
```

45

In summary, the main difference between **CHAR** and **VARCHAR** in SQL is that **CHAR** stores fixed-length strings with padding, while **VARCHAR** stores variable-length strings without padding.

The choice between the two data types depends on the nature of the data being stored and the expected lengths of the strings. If you have data with consistent lengths, **CHAR** might be more suitable, whereas for variable-length data, **VARCHAR** is generally a better choice due to its efficient use of storage.

Question 17

Difference between VARCHAR and NVARCHAR in SQL Server?

Short answer - NVARCHAR supports Unicode while VARCHAR doesn't

Long answer - In SQL Server, **VARCHAR** and **NVARCHAR** are both used to store character data, but they differ in how they handle character encoding. **VARCHAR** stores data using the database's default encoding (e.g., ASCII or UTF-8), while **NVARCHAR** uses a variable-length Unicode encoding (UTF-16), allowing storage of multi-byte characters. **NVARCHAR** is ideal for internationalization and multilingual data, but it consumes more storage space than **VARCHAR**. Use **VARCHAR** for single-byte character sets and **NVARCHAR** for multi-byte character sets to ensure proper handling of character data in the database.

Question 18

How do you get Day, Month, and Year from a date in SQL Server?

Short answer - By using the DATEPART() function

Long answer - In SQL Server, you can extract the day, month, and year components from a date using various built-in functions. Here's how you can do it:

1. **Get Day:** To extract the day from a date, you can use the **DAY()** function. It returns the day of the month as an integer value ranging from 1 to 31.

```
SELECT DAY(your_date_column) AS DayValue
FROM your_table;
```

1. **Get Month:** To extract the month from a date, you can use the **MONTH()** function. It returns the month as an integer value ranging from 1 to 12.

```
SELECT MONTH(your_date_column) AS MonthValue
FROM your_table;
```

1. **Get Year:** To extract the year from a date, you can use the **YEAR()** function. It returns the year as an integer value.

```
SELECT YEAR(your_date_column) AS YearValue
FROM your_table;
```

Just replace **your_date_column** with the actual column name containing the date you want to extract the components from, and **your_table** with the appropriate table name. The result will give you the day, month, and year components of the date in separate columns.

Question 19

How to check if a date is valid in SQL?

In SQL, you can check if a date is valid using the **TRY_CAST()** or **TRY_CONVERT()** function.

These functions attempt to convert the input expression to the specified data type and return NULL if the conversion fails.

To check if a date is valid, you can try to cast or convert the date string to a date data type (e.g., **DATE, DATETIME, SMALLDATETIME**, etc.).

47

If the conversion is successful, the date is valid; otherwise, it will return NULL.

Here's an example using **TRY_CAST()** to check if a date string is valid:

```
DECLARE @dateString VARCHAR(50) = '2023-08-04';

IF TRY_CAST(@dateString AS DATE) IS NOT NULL
BEGIN
    PRINT 'Valid Date';
END
ELSE
BEGIN
    PRINT 'Invalid Date';
END
```

In this example, **TRY_CAST()** attempts to convert the **@dateString** to a **DATE** data type. If the conversion is successful, it means the date is valid, and the code inside the **IF** block will be executed. Otherwise, it will go to the **ELSE** block, indicating that the date is invalid.

You can also use **TRY_CONVERT()** function in a similar manner:

```
DECLARE @dateString VARCHAR(50) = '2023-08-04';

IF TRY_CONVERT(DATE, @dateString) IS NOT NULL
BEGIN
    PRINT 'Valid Date';
END
ELSE
BEGIN
    PRINT 'Invalid Date';
END
```

Both **TRY_CAST()** and **TRY_CONVERT()** are helpful when dealing with user inputs or data from external sources, as they provide a safe way to handle date conversions and check for valid dates.

Question 20

Difference between LEFT OUTER JOIN and INNER JOIN in SQL?

In SQL, both **LEFT OUTER JOIN** and **INNER JOIN** are used to combine data from two or more tables, but they produce different results:

1. INNER JOIN: An **INNER JOIN** returns only the rows that have matching values in both tables based on the specified join condition. It effectively filters out rows where there is no match in the joined table. In other words, an **INNER JOIN** produces a result set that contains only the rows with matching keys in both tables.

<u>Example:</u>

```
SELECT employees.name, departments.department_name
FROM employees
INNER JOIN departments ON employees.department_id = departments.department_i
```

In this example, only the rows where there is a match between the **employees** table and the **departments** table on the **department_id** column will be returned.

1. LEFT OUTER JOIN: A **LEFT OUTER JOIN** returns all the rows from the left (first) table and the matching rows from the right (second) table. If there is no match in the right table, NULL values will be returned for columns from the right table. It keeps all the rows from the left table regardless of whether there is a matching row in the right table.

<u>Example:</u>

```
SELECT customers.name, orders.order_id
FROM customers
LEFT OUTER JOIN orders ON customers.customer_id = orders.customer_id;
```

Question 21

What is SELF JOIN in SQL?

When we join two instances of tables it's called self-join. For example, if the table contains employee name and role then you can use self-joincopy to find all employees who are managers.

Question 22

In a classical Employee and Department relationship, write SQL query to print all departments and number of employees on each department.

To print all departments along with the number of employees in each department, you can use a **LEFT OUTER JOIN** and the **COUNT()** function. Assuming you have two tables named **departments** and **employees** with a foreign key **department_id** in the **employees** table that references the **department_id** in the **departments** table, you can use the following SQL query:

```
SELECT d.department_name, COUNT(e.employee_id) AS num_of_employees
FROM departments d
LEFT OUTER JOIN employees e ON d.department_id = e.department_id
GROUP BY d.department_name;
```

Explanation:

1. We start with the **departments** table, aliasing it as **d**, and then perform a **LEFT OUTER JOIN** with the **employees** table, aliasing it as **e**, using the common column **department_id**.

50

2. The **LEFT OUTER JOIN** ensures that all departments from the **departments** table are included in the result, even if there are no matching employees in the **employees** table.

3. We use the **COUNT(e.employee_id)** function to count the number of employees for each department. The **COUNT()** function will only count non-NULL values, so it will accurately count the number of employees in each department.

4. The **GROUP BY d.department_name** groups the result by department name, so we get the count of employees for each department.

The query will provide a result set with two columns: **department_name** and **num_of_employees**, showing all departments and the corresponding number of employees in each department.

Question 23

Difference between COUNT(*), COUNT(1), and COUNT(column_ name) in SQL?

Short answer - COUNT(*) includes null values while counting but COUNT(1), and COUNT(column_name) doesn't take null values into consideration during counting.

Long answer:

In SQL, **COUNT(*)**, **COUNT(1)**, and **COUNT(column_name)** are all used with the **COUNT()** aggregate function to count the number of rows in a result set or the number of non-null values in a specific column. However, they have slight differences in their behavior:

1. COUNT(*):

- **COUNT(*)** counts the total number of rows in the result set, including rows with NULL values in all columns.

- It does not consider individual column values but simply counts the rows that satisfy the conditions in the query.

- It is usually the fastest option for counting rows because it does not involve evaluating any column values.

Example:

```
SELECT COUNT(*) AS total_rows FROM employees;
```

2. COUNT(1):

- **COUNT(1)** is similar to **COUNT(*)**, as it also counts the total number of rows in the result set, including rows with NULL values in all columns.
- Instead of considering individual column values, it uses the constant value "1" for each row in the result set, effectively counting the rows without evaluating any column values.
- Like **COUNT(*)**, it is a fast option for counting rows.

Example:

```
SELECT COUNT(1) AS total_rows FROM employees;
```

3. COUNT(column_name):

- **COUNT(column_name)** counts the number of non-null values in the specified column. It excludes rows with NULL values in the specified column from the count.
- It is used when you want to count the occurrences of non-null values in a particular column.

Example:

```
SELECT COUNT(employee_id) AS non_null_employee_ids
FROM employees;
```

In summary, **COUNT(*)** and **COUNT(1)** are used to count all rows in the result set, while **COUNT(column_name)** is used to count the non-null values in a specific column. All three options have their specific use cases, and the choice depends on what you want to count in your SQL query. For counting all rows, **COUNT(*)** is the most commonly used and efficient option.

Question 24

What is Database statistics? How it affects the performance of your Query?

One of the first thing I do when my app become slow is to update the statistics on DB. It immediately boost the performance for one reason or other.

Database statistics refer to the information and metrics about the data distribution and structure within a database. These statistics are typically collected and maintained by the database management system (DBMS) and are used **by the query optimizer** to determine the most efficient execution plan for a given SQL query.

When you execute a query in a database, the query optimizer's role is to analyze various possible execution plans and choose the one that is likely to result in the fastest and most efficient execution. The optimizer relies heavily on database statistics to make these decisions.

How Database Statistics Affect Query Performance:

1. **Query Plan Selection:** The query optimizer uses statistics to estimate the number of rows that will be returned by each step of the query execution plan. It then evaluates various possible plans and selects the one with the lowest estimated cost. Accurate statistics lead to better choices of query plans and, therefore, faster query execution.

2. **Index Selection**: Database statistics help the optimizer determine which indexes are the most selective for a given query. A more selective index reduces the number of rows that need to be scanned, leading to faster data retrieval.

3. **Join Order:** In queries with multiple tables, the optimizer needs to decide the order in which to join the tables. Statistics on table sizes and data distribution are crucial in making the most efficient join order decisions.

4. **Predicate Evaluation**: Statistics allow the optimizer to estimate the selectivity of various predicates in the query's

WHERE clause. This helps in determining which parts of the query filter out the most data, guiding the optimizer to create more efficient execution plans.

5. **Memory and Resource Allocation**: Accurate statistics help the optimizer estimate the memory and resources required for query execution. This enables the DBMS to allocate appropriate resources for optimal performance.

As I said, regularly updating statistics is important to maintain the query performance, especially in databases with large amounts of data that undergo frequent data changes (inserts, updates, and deletes). Outdated or inaccurate statistics may cause the optimizer to generate suboptimal query execution plans, leading to performance degradation.

Database administrators can use database-specific commands or built-in functions to update statistics periodically or automatically to ensure the optimizer has the most up-to-date information for query optimization.

Pro tip

if you run import jobs make sure you include a command to update the statistics after data is imported like

```
UPDATE STATISTICS table_name [ {
index_or_statistics_name } ]
```

Question 25

Suppose you have to create a compound index in a table, involving two columns like book_id and active. Now you can create them as either (book_id, active) or (active, book_id), do you think the order of columns in an index matter? How it will affect your SQL queries?

Yes, the order of columns in a compound index can matter, and it can significantly affect the performance of SQL queries. The order of columns in an index impacts how the index is utilized by the query optimizer for different types of queries.

When creating a compound index involving two columns like **book_id** and **active**, the choice of the order of these columns can lead to different index structures and query optimizations:

1. (book_id, active) Index: This index order is more suitable when queries frequently involve filtering by **book_id** and then further filter by **active**. For example, if you have queries like:

```
SELECT * FROM books WHERE book_id = ? AND active = 1;
```

In this case, the **(book_id, active)** index can be highly effective, as it can quickly locate the rows with the specific **book_id** and then further narrow down the results based on the **active** status.

1. (active, book_id) Index: On the other hand, this index order is more appropriate when queries often involve filtering by active and then by book_id. For example, if you have queries like:

```
SELECT * FROM books WHERE active = 1 AND book_id = ?;
```

In this scenario, the **(active, book_id)** index would be more efficient, as it can quickly find the rows with the desired **active** status and then further filter by **book_id**.

Keep in mind that the order of columns in the index should be based on the query patterns and the filtering conditions you expect to see in your application. In some cases, it might be beneficial to create multiple indexes with different column orders to optimize different query patterns.

However, **creating too many indexes can also have downsides,** such as increased storage and maintenance overhead, so it's essential to strike a balance and consider the most common and performance-critical query scenarios when designing compound indexes.

Question 26

What do _ and % are used in the SQL query?

Short answer - They are used in the LIKE operators while writing SQL queries. The underscore is used to match one character, while % is used for any number of characters.

Long Answer - In SQL queries, both _ (underscore) and % (percent sign) are special characters used in conjunction with the LIKE operator in the WHERE clause for pattern matching in string comparisons.

1. **Underscore (_) Wildcard**: The underscore (_) is used as a wildcard that represents any single character. When used in a **LIKE** comparison, it matches exactly one character at the position where it appears.

For example, suppose you want to find all names that start with "J" and have exactly four characters in total:

```
SELECT * FROM employees WHERE name LIKE 'J___';
```

This query will retrieve all records where the name starts with "J" and has exactly four characters after the initial "J."

1. **Percent Sign (%) Wildcard:** The percent sign (%) is used as a wildcard that represents any sequence of characters (including zero characters). When used in a **LIKE** comparison, it matches any number of characters, including none, at the position where it appears.

For example, suppose you want to find all names that start with "A":

```
SELECT * FROM employees WHERE name LIKE 'A%';
```

This query will retrieve all records where the name starts with "A," followed by any sequence of characters.

You can also use the **%** wildcard in combination with other characters to create more complex patterns. For instance, **%n%** will match any name that contains the letter "n" at any position.

Keep in mind that the **LIKE** operator is not case-sensitive by default in most database systems. If you need case-sensitive matching, you can use appropriate collations or convert the strings to a specific case using functions like **LOWER()** or **UPPER()** before performing the comparison.

Question 27

How do you ensure that a particular SQL query will use a particular Index?

Short answer - You can use SQL hints for that purpose.

Long answer - In SQL, you cannot directly force a query to use a specific index. The query optimizer in the database management system (DBMS) is responsible for choosing the most efficient execution plan, including which indexes to use, based on the available statistics and the complexity of the query.

However, **you can influence the query optimizer's decision and encourage it to use a particular index** by following these best practices:

- **Create the Right Index:** Ensure that you have appropriate indexes on the columns used in the query's **WHERE**, **JOIN**, and **ORDER BY** clauses. The presence of a suitable index increases the chances of the query optimizer selecting it.

- **Statistics:** Keep the statistics up-to-date for the tables and indexes. The query optimizer relies on statistics to estimate the cost of different execution plans and make informed decisions.

- **Index Hints:** Some database systems provide index hints that allow you to suggest which index to use in a query. However, using hints should be a last resort, as the query optimizer is generally good at choosing efficient execution plans.

- **Rewrite the Query:** Sometimes, rewriting the query can influence the query optimizer's choices. Small changes in the query logic might lead to different execution plans, which may make better use of certain indexes.

- **Covering Indexes:** Create covering indexes that include all the columns required by the query. This allows the query to retrieve all the necessary data directly from the index without accessing the actual table, improving performance.

- **Avoid Indexing Overkill:** Having too many indexes on a table can increase the overhead of maintaining them and might confuse the query optimizer. Keep indexes selective and remove unused or redundant indexes.

- Remember that the **query optimizer's decision to use an index is based on the overall cost estimation for the execution plan**. Even if you encourage the use of a specific index, the optimizer may still choose a different index or even perform a full table scan if it deems it more efficient. Trust the optimizer's capabilities, and focus on providing the right indexes and maintaining up-to-date statistics to help it make informed choices. Only consider using index hints as a last resort and after thorough performance testing to ensure that they indeed improve query performance.

Question 28

In SQL Server, which one is fastest and slowest between an index seek, an index scan, and table scan?

Short answer - In a general, the table scan is slower than the index scan and index seek. Your goal should be to write queries that can take advantage of the index by using index scan and index seek for faster retrieval. You can use the SQL EXPLAIN command to retrieve the query plans and find out whether indexes are used for your query or not.

Long answer - In SQL Server, the speed of an operation varies *depending on the size of the data and the specific query being executed.* However, in general, the fastest operation is an Index Seek, followed by an Index Scan, and the slowest operation is a Table Scan.

1. Index Seek:

- An **Index Seek** is the fastest operation because it directly navigates to the specific rows in the table using the index key. It is efficient for queries that have selective criteria, as it minimizes the number of rows to be retrieved.

2. Index Scan:

- An **Index Scan** is the second fastest operation. It reads all the rows in an index (or a range of index entries) that match the query's filter conditions. While not as efficient as an **Index Seek**, it is still faster than a **Table Scan** because it involves reading only a subset of data from the index.

3. Table Scan:

- A **Table Scan** is the slowest operation. It reads all the rows from a table, whether or not they match the query's filter conditions. It is the least efficient operation, as it involves reading the entire table, which can be very time-consuming for large tables.

The performance of these operations can be influenced by factors such as the size of the table, the distribution of data, the presence of suitable indexes, and the complexity of the query. It's essential to create appropriate indexes and write efficient queries to ensure that SQL Server can use **Index Seeks** and **Index Scans** whenever possible, as they are more efficient than **Table Scans**.

The SQL Server query optimizer plays a crucial role in determining which operation to use based on statistics, available indexes, and query complexity. By ensuring proper indexing and writing well-optimized queries, you can improve query performance and reduce the likelihood of **Table Scans**, which tend to be the slowest operation.

Question 29

What does NULL = NULL will return in SQL?

In SQL, the expression **NULL = NULL** will *not* return **TRUE**, as you might expect. Instead, it will return **NULL**.

The reason for this behaviour is that **NULL** represents an unknown or missing value, and SQL uses a three-valued logic system where the result of comparisons involving **NULL** can be **TRUE, FALSE**, or **NULL**.

When you compare two **NULL** values using the equals (=) operator, SQL cannot determine whether they are equal or not because they are both unknown. As a result, the comparison returns **NULL** as an indicator of uncertainty.

To check for **NULL** values in SQL, you should use the **IS NULL** or **IS NOT NULL** operators:

- **IS NULL**: Used to check if a value is **NULL**.
- **IS NOT NULL**: Used to check if a value is not **NULL**.

For example:

```
SELECT *
FROM employees
WHERE department_id IS NULL;
```

In this query, we are selecting all records from the **employees** table where the **department_id** column has a **NULL** value. This is the correct way to handle **NULL** comparisons in SQL.

Question 30

Write SQL query to find all rows where EMP_NAME, a VARCHAR column is NULL?

This is a simple question often asked beginners to check whether they know how to check for NULL in SQL or not. The trick here is to use "IS NULL" instead of the "=" operator to find all rows where EMP_NAME is NULL.

Here is the SQL query for this

```
SELECT EMP_NAME
FROM Employee
WHERE EMP_NAME IS NULL;
```

Question 31

What is the temp table?

Short answer - A temp table or a temporary table is a base table that is not stored in the database and only exists while the current database session is active. Once the database connection is closed, **all temp tables are lost.** They may look similar to view but they are not. A view exists only for a single query but you can use a temporary table as a regular table until your session is active.

Long answer - A temporary table, often referred to as a "temp table," is a special type of table that exists only for the duration of a database session or transaction. Temporary tables are commonly used to store intermediate results or temporary data during the execution of complex queries or stored procedures.There are two main types of temporary tables:

1. Local Temporary Table:

- A local temporary table is created using a single "#" symbol before the table name (e.g., **#temp_table**). It is visible only within the session or connection that created it.

61

- Once the session or connection that created the local temporary table is closed or disconnected, the table is automatically dropped, and its data is lost.

2. Global Temporary Table:

- A global temporary table is created using a double "##" symbol before the table name (e.g., **##temp_table**). It is visible across different sessions or connections within the same database.

- The global temporary table persists until all sessions that have referenced it are closed or disconnected. Once the last session using the global temporary table ends, the table is automatically dropped, and its data is lost.

Temporary tables offer several benefits:

- They can improve query performance by allowing the storage of intermediate results during complex operations.
- Temporary tables can be used to break down complex tasks into smaller, more manageable steps.
- They provide isolation for each session, so different users or applications can use temporary tables independently without interfering with each other's data.
- Temporary tables can be used to store temporary data for reporting or data manipulation tasks.

However, it's essential to use temporary tables judiciously, as they consume resources and can impact database performance if not managed properly. Ensure that you drop temporary tables when they are no longer needed to avoid unnecessary resource usage. Additionally, temporary tables are typically not recommended for long-term data storage or as a replacement for permanent tables in the database schema.

Question 32

What is the fastest way to empty or clear a table?

Short answer - You can use the `truncate` command to empty or clear the table. It's faster than `delete` because it doesn't log each deleted entry on a log, that's why you cannot roll back it. So be careful while using truncate to clear or empty a table.

Long answer - The fastest way to empty or clear a table in most relational database systems, including SQL Server, is to use the **TRUNCATE TABLE** statement. The **TRUNCATE TABLE** statement removes all rows from a table quickly and efficiently, and it is typically faster than using the **DELETE** statement, especially for large tables.

Here's the syntax for the **TRUNCATE TABLE** statement:

```
TRUNCATE TABLE table_name;
```

Replace **table_name** with the name of the table you want to empty.

Advantages of using **TRUNCATE TABLE** over **DELETE**:

- **Speed: TRUNCATE TABLE** is faster because it does not generate individual row delete operations and does not log individual row deletions. It deallocates the data pages of the table directly, resulting in quicker completion.

- **Minimal Logging: TRUNCATE TABLE** is a minimally logged operation. In most cases, it only logs the deallocation of the data pages, making it faster and consuming less transaction log space than **DELETE**.

- **No Rollback: TRUNCATE TABLE** cannot be rolled back, which is an advantage in situations where you want to quickly remove all data from the table without the possibility of reverting the operation.

However, there are a few important considerations when using **TRUNCATE TABLE**:

- **Cannot be used with Referential Integrity**: You cannot use **TRUNCATE TABLE** on a table that has foreign key constraints referencing it. In such cases, you would need to use **DELETE** or remove the foreign key constraints temporarily.

- **Resets Identity Columns:** If the table has an identity column, using **TRUNCATE TABLE** will reset the identity seed back to its original starting value. Be cautious if you have other tables referencing this identity value.

- **Requires Appropriate Permissions**: Ensure that you have the necessary permissions to truncate the table, as this operation is a powerful one that clears all data.

In summary, if you need to quickly empty or clear a table and you don't have foreign key constraints referencing it, the **TRUNCATE TABLE** statement is the fastest and most efficient option. However, be mindful of the considerations mentioned above and verify that it aligns with your specific use case.

Question 33

What is an identity column in SQL Server? How do you return an identity value from a table?

In SQL Server, an identity column is a special type of column that automatically generates a unique value for each new row added to a table. It is commonly used to provide a unique and sequential identifier for the rows in a table. The values in an identity column are typically used as primary keys for the table.

To define an identity column in SQL Server, you use the **IDENTITY** property in the **CREATE TABLE** statement or alter an existing column using the **ALTER TABLE** statement.

Here's the syntax for creating an identity column:

```
CREATE TABLE your_table
(
    column_name data_type PRIMARY KEY IDENTITY(1,1),
    -- Other columns...
);
```

In this example, **column_name** is the name of the column you want to define as an identity column. **data_type** is the data type of the column, and **PRIMARY KEY** indicates that the identity column will be the primary key for the table. The **IDENTITY(1,1)** specifies the seed value and the increment value for the identity column. In this case, the identity starts at 1 and increments by 1 for each new row.

To return the identity value from a table after inserting a new row, you can use one of the following methods:

1. **@@IDENTITY**: The **@@IDENTITY** system function returns the last generated identity value in the current session and current scope. It is essential to be cautious with **@@IDENTITY** when there are triggers or other operations that may affect the identity value. It might not return the value you expect in certain scenarios.

```
INSERT INTO your_table (column1, column2, ...)
VALUES (value1, value2, ...);

SELECT @@IDENTITY AS last_identity;
```

1. **SCOPE_IDENTITY ()**: The **SCOPE_IDENTITY ()** function returns the last generated identity value within the current scope, but it takes into account triggers. It is generally considered safer and more reliable than **@@IDENTITY**.

```
INSERT INTO your_table (column1, column2, ...)
VALUES (value1, value2, ...);

SELECT SCOPE_IDENTITY() AS last_identity;
```

1. **OUTPUT** Clause: The **OUTPUT** clause can be used with the **INSERT** statement to return the identity value(s) of the inserted row(s) directly in the query result.

```
DECLARE @OutputTable TABLE (column_name data_type);

INSERT INTO your_table (column1, column2, ...)
OUTPUT inserted.column_name INTO @OutputTable
VALUES (value1, value2, ...);

SELECT * FROM @OutputTable;
```

You should choose the appropriate method based on your specific use case and the behaviour you need for returning the identity value after an insert operation.

Question 34

How do you return an identity value from a table with a trigger?

Short answer - In SQL Server, you can use a function like @@IDENTITY to generate identity values.

```
Example - SELECT @@IDENTITY AS 'Identity';
```

Long answer – see previous questions

Question 35

How do you return a value from a stored procedure?

Short answer - In SQL Server, you can either use the OUTPUT parameter or use the return statement to return a value from a stored procedure.

Long answer - In SQL Server, you can return a value from a stored procedure using the RETURN statement or by using an OUTPUT parameter.

1. Using the RETURN Statement:

The **RETURN** statement is used to return an integer value from a stored procedure. This value is typically used to indicate the status of the procedure execution. By convention, a value of 0 indicates successful execution, and non-zero values indicate various error conditions.

Here's an example of a stored procedure that uses the **RETURN** statement:

```
CREATE PROCEDURE dbo.GetEmployeeCount
AS
BEGIN
    DECLARE @EmployeeCount INT;
    -- Perform some logic to calculate the employee count
    SET @EmployeeCount = (SELECT COUNT(*) FROM Employees);

    -- Return the employee count as the result of the stored procedure
    RETURN @EmployeeCount;
END;
```

To execute the stored procedure and retrieve the returned value, you use the following:

```
DECLARE @Result INT;
EXEC @Result = dbo.GetEmployeeCount;
PRINT @Result;
```

2. Using OUTPUT Parameters:

OUTPUT parameters are used to pass values from a stored procedure back to the calling code. Unlike the **RETURN** statement, you can use **OUTPUT** parameters to return multiple values from a stored procedure.

Here's an example of a stored procedure with an **OUTPUT** parameter:

```
CREATE PROCEDURE dbo.GetEmployeeDetails
    @EmployeeID INT,
    @EmployeeName NVARCHAR(50) OUTPUT,
    @Department NVARCHAR(50) OUTPUT
AS
BEGIN
    -- Perform some logic to retrieve employee details
    SELECT @EmployeeName = Name, @Department = Department
    FROM Employees
    WHERE EmployeeID = @EmployeeID;
END;
```

```
CREATE PROCEDURE dbo.GetEmployeeDetails
    @EmployeeID INT,
    @EmployeeName NVARCHAR(50) OUTPUT,
    @Department NVARCHAR(50) OUTPUT
AS
BEGIN
    -- Perform some logic to retrieve employee details
    SELECT @EmployeeName = Name, @Department = Department
    FROM Employees
    WHERE EmployeeID = @EmployeeID;
END;
```

To execute the stored procedure and retrieve the values returned through **OUTPUT** parameters, you use the following:

```
DECLARE @Name NVARCHAR(50), @Dept NVARCHAR(50);
EXEC dbo.GetEmployeeDetails
    @EmployeeID = 1,
    @EmployeeName = @Name OUTPUT,
    @Department = @Dept OUTPUT;


PRINT @Name;
PRINT @Dept;
```

Remember that **RETURN** statements can only return a single integer value, while **OUTPUT** parameters can return multiple values of different data types. Choose the appropriate method based on the number and type of values you need to return from the stored procedure.

Question 36

How do you return a VARCHAR value from a stored procedure?

Hint - using OUTPUT parameter return clause as shown above

Question 37

If you have a column that will only have values between 1 and 250 what data type will you use?

If you are using SQL Server database then you can use the TINYINT datatype which can accommodate numbers between 0 and 255 and it needs 1 byte for storage.

This question is asked to test your knowledge of SQL data type and whether you can choose the right data type for a given requirement or not. Your goal should be to use a data type that can accommodate a given range. You can also ask questions that whether it's fixed or it can change in the future.

Question 38

Difference between LEFT and RIGHT OUTER JOIN in SQL?

Both are outer joins, in LEFT outer join, **all rows from the left side table will be included**, and only matching rows from the other side of the table are included. In case of RIGHT outer join, all rows of the right side of the table on join condition are included.

Question 39

Can you write an SQL query to select all last names that start with 'T'?

Here's an SQL query to select all last names that start with 'T':

```
SELECT last_name
FROM employees
WHERE last_name LIKE 'T%';
```

In this query:

1. The **SELECT** statement retrieves the **last_name** column from the **employees** table.
2. The **WHERE** clause filters the results to include only rows where the **last_name** starts with the letter 'T'. The **LIKE**

'**T%**' condition specifies that the **last_name** should begin with 'T', followed by any characters.

This query will return all last names that start with the letter 'T' from the **employees** table.

Question 40

How would you select all rows where the date is 20231002?

To select all rows where the date is '2023-10-02', you would use the following SQL query:

```
SELECT *
FROM your_table
WHERE date_column = '2023-10-02';
```

Replace **your_table** with the actual name of your table and **date_column** with the name of the column that holds the date values.

This query will retrieve all rows from the specified table where the date in the **date_column** is '2023-10-02'.

Question 41

What is the difference between a local and global temporary table in SQL Server?

I did explained this before on previous question but here it is again:

In SQL Server, local and global temporary tables are two types of temporary tables that serve different purposes:

1. Local Temporary Table:

- Local temporary tables are created using a single hash (#) sign as a prefix in their name (e.g., **#temp_table**).
- They are only visible and accessible within the current session (connection) that creates them.

- Local temporary tables are automatically dropped when the session that created them is closed or when the user explicitly drops them.
- They are useful for temporary data storage within a specific session, such as in stored procedures or user-defined functions.

2. Global Temporary Table:

- Global temporary tables are created using a double hash (##) sign as a prefix in their name (e.g., **##temp_table**).
- They are visible and accessible across multiple sessions and connections within the same database.
- Global temporary tables are automatically dropped when the last session that references them is closed or when the user explicitly drops them.
- They are suitable for scenarios where temporary data needs to be shared among multiple sessions or connections, such as in complex queries or data manipulation tasks.

In summary, the main differences between local and global temporary tables lie in their scope and lifespan. Local temporary tables are limited to a single session and are dropped when the session ends, while global temporary tables can be accessed by multiple sessions and are dropped when the last session that references them is closed.

Question 42

How do you create a copy of a table in SQL Server?

To create a copy of a table in SQL Server, you can use various methods, depending on your requirements and the complexity of the table structure. Here are a few approaches:

1. Using SELECT INTO Statement:

```
SELECT * INTO new_table FROM old_table;
```

This creates a new table **new_table** with the same structure as **old_table** and copies all data into it.

2. *Using INSERT INTO Statement:*

```
INSERT INTO new_table SELECT * FROM old_table;
```

This inserts all data from **old_table** into an existing **new_table**.

Question 43

How do you change the data type of a column in a table in SQL?

To change the data type of a column in a table in SQL, you can use the ALTER TABLE statement along with the ALTER COLUMN clause. Here's the general syntax:

```
ALTER TABLE table_name ALTER COLUMN column_name
new_data_type;
```

Replace table_name with the name of the table containing the column, column_name with the name of the column you want to modify, and new_data_type with the desired new data type.

For example, if you want to change the data type of a column named age in a table named employees to INT, the SQL statement would be:

```
ALTER TABLE employees ALTER COLUMN age INT;
```

Keep in mind the following considerations:

1. **Data Conversion:** Changing data types might result in data loss or truncation if the new data type cannot accommodate the existing data.

2. **Constraints and Indexes**: If the column has constraints, indexes, or other dependent objects, you might need to drop and recreate them after altering the column's data type.

3. **Potential Downtime**: Depending on the database system and the amount of data, changing a data type can require significant processing time and might cause downtime for the table.

4. **Testing**: Always perform such operations in a controlled environment, and it's a good practice to back up your data before making significant changes.

5. **Impacted Queries**: Changing a column's data type might affect queries, so be sure to review and update any affected parts of your application.

Make sure to review the documentation for your specific database system to understand any nuances or limitations related to altering column data types.

Question 44

What data type should you use to store monetary values in a table?

When storing monetary values in a table, it is recommended to use the **DECIMAL** (also known as **NUMERIC**) data type. This data type is specifically designed for precise decimal arithmetic and is suitable for representing fixed-point numbers, such as monetary values.

In SQL Server, the **DECIMAL** data type requires two parameters:

1. Precision (**p**): The total number of digits that can be stored, both to the left and right of the decimal point.

2. Scale (**s**): The number of decimal places that are stored to the right of the decimal point.

For example, if you want to store monetary values with up to 10 digits in total and up to 2 decimal places, you might define the column as **DECIMAL(10, 2)**.

Here's an example of creating a table with a column to store monetary values:

```
CREATE TABLE FinancialData (
    TransactionID INT PRIMARY KEY,
    Amount DECIMAL(10, 2)
);
```

Using the **DECIMAL** data type ensures accurate representation of monetary values and helps prevent rounding errors that can occur with floating-point data types like **FLOAT** or **REAL**.

Question 45

What does SELECT 3/2 will return? 1 or 1.5?

In most programming languages including Java and database systems, including SQL Server, when you perform an arithmetic operation like division on integers, the result is treated as an integer division, and any fractional part is truncated (rounded down).

So, in the case of **SELECT 3/2**, the result will be **1**, not **1.5**. The fractional part **0.5** is truncated, and only the integer part of the division result is returned.

If you want to perform a division that results in a decimal or floating-point value, you should use decimal or floating-point literals or variables, like **SELECT 3.0 / 2** or **SELECT 3 / 2.0**, which will give you the result **1.5**.

Question 46

What is the maximum value that Decimal (6, 5) can hold in SQL Server?

In SQL Server, the **Decimal (p, s)** data type represents a fixed precision and scale decimal number. The **p** parameter specifies the total number of digits that the number can hold (precision), and the **s** parameter specifies the number of decimal places (scale).

For **Decimal (6, 5)**, this means it can hold a total of 6 digits, with 5 of those digits being reserved for decimal places. The remaining digit is used for the non-decimal part.

The maximum value that a **Decimal (6, 5)** can hold is determined by its precision and scale. In this case, with a precision of 6 and a scale of 5, the maximum value can be represented as:

0.99999

This value is derived from the fact that there are 6 total digits, with 5 of them after the decimal point. The largest value that can be represented is where all the available digits are set to 9 in the decimal places.

Please note that the actual range of values might be constrained by other factors such as the available memory and storage.

Question 47

If you have a table with one integer column ID, and it has three values 101, 201, and NULL? What will the following SQL query SELECT * FROM TestTable where ID !=101 will return?

The SQL query **SELECT * FROM TestTable WHERE ID != 101** will return the rows where the **ID** column is not equal to 101. However, it's important to note that when comparing with NULL values, the result might not be as straightforward as expected due to the three-valued logic used in SQL (True, False, and Unknown).

Given the table with values 101, 201, and NULL:

- **101** is not equal to **101** (False)
- **201** is not equal to **101** (True)
- **NULL** is not equal to **101** is evaluated as Unknown

So, the result of the query will be:

- One row with **ID = 201**

Rows with NULL values are not included in the result set because comparisons involving NULL values often result in Unknown, and rows for which the comparison result is Unknown are not included in the output according to SQL's three-valued logic.

Question 48

What is your favorite SQL book?

This one is an easy question and the interviewer just wants to know whether you have read any book or not. You can name the SQL book you have read, if you haven't read any SQL book so far then I highly recommend you to read Head First SQL if you are learning SQL from scratch and Joe **Celko's SQL Puzzles if** you already know SQL and looking for some SQL puzzles to test your SQL query skills.

Question 49

Tell me two SQL best practices you follow?

Short answer - creating indexes and using them on SQL queries, normalization, and updating statistics regularly.

Long answer – Here are two SQL best practices that are widely recommended:

1. **Parameterized Queries:** Always use parameterized queries or prepared statements to prevent SQL injection attacks. Instead of embedding user inputs directly into SQL statements, pass them as parameters. Parameterization not only safeguards your database from malicious input but also improves query performance by allowing the database to cache query plans. Example in SQL Server using T-SQL:

```
DECLARE @Username NVARCHAR(50);
SET @Username = 'user123';

SELECT * FROM Users WHERE Username = @Username;
```

1. **Use Indexes Wisely:** Employ appropriate indexes on columns that are frequently used in search, join, or filter operations. Indexes enhance query performance by reducing the need for full table scans. However, avoid excessive indexing, as it can lead to increased storage

requirements and slower write operations. Regularly monitor and analyse query execution plans to ensure that indexes are being used effectively. Example:

```
CREATE INDEX idx_LastName ON Employees(LastName);
```

By following these best practices, you can improve the security, performance, and maintainability of your SQL code and database systems.

Question 50

What is the different ISOLATION level in the Microsoft SQL Server database?

In Microsoft SQL Server, isolation levels define how transactions interact with each other in a multi-user environment. Different isolation levels provide varying degrees of transaction isolation and concurrency control. Here are the standard isolation levels available in SQL Server:

1. READ UNCOMMITTED:

- Least restrictive isolation level.
- Allows transactions to read uncommitted changes made by other transactions, leading to potential dirty reads, non-repeatable reads, and phantom reads.

2. READ COMMITTED:

- Default isolation level.
- Allows transactions to read only committed data, avoiding dirty reads. However, it may still experience non-repeatable reads and phantom reads.

3. REPEATABLE READ:

- Prevents other transactions from updating or inserting new rows that would affect the result set of the current transaction.

- Guarantees consistent results for read operations, but can still lead to phantom reads (newly inserted rows).

4. SERIALIZABLE:

- Provides the highest level of isolation.

- Prevents other transactions from updating, inserting, or deleting rows that would affect the result set of the current transaction.

- Offers the highest data integrity but can lead to decreased concurrency due to locking.

5. SNAPSHOT:

- Uses row versioning to allow each transaction to see a snapshot of the data as it existed at the start of the transaction.

- Helps to prevent blocking and provides a higher level of concurrency than SERIALIZABLE.

6. READ COMMITTED SNAPSHOT:

- Similar to READ COMMITTED, but uses row versioning to avoid blocking.

- Provides a balance between isolation and concurrency.

Isolation levels affect how locks are acquired and released, impacting the trade-off between data consistency and concurrency. Choosing the appropriate isolation level depends on the specific requirements of your application and the potential impact on performance and concurrency. It's important to carefully consider the implications of each isolation level and test their behaviour in your specific use case.

Question 51

If you create a local temp table and then call a proc is the temp table available inside the proc?

Yes, if you create a local temporary table (**#table_name**) and then call a stored procedure in the same session, the temporary table will be available inside the stored procedure.

Local temporary tables are session-specific, meaning they are accessible only within the context of the session that created them, including any stored procedures called from that session.

Here's an example scenario:

```sql
-- Create a local temporary table
CREATE TABLE #TempTable (
    ID INT,
    Name VARCHAR(50)
);

-- Insert data into the temporary table
INSERT INTO #TempTable (ID, Name) VALUES (1, 'John'), (2, 'Jane');

-- Call a stored procedure that uses the temporary table
EXEC YourStoredProcedure;

-- Stored procedure definition
CREATE PROCEDURE YourStoredProcedure
AS
BEGIN
    -- The temporary table is accessible here
    SELECT * FROM #TempTable;
END;
```

In this example, the temporary table **#TempTable** is created in the main session, data is inserted into it, and then the stored procedure **YourStoredProcedure** is called.

Inside the stored procedure, the temporary table is still accessible, and you can perform operations on it.

Remember that local temporary tables are automatically dropped when the session that created them ends.

This means that after the session ends (when the connection is closed), the temporary table will no longer exist.

Question 52

Which date format is the only safe one to use when passing dates as strings?

When passing dates as strings in SQL queries, the safest date format to use is the ISO 8601 format, specifically the "YYYY-MM-DD" format for dates and "YYYY-MM-DDTHH:MM:SS" format for timestamps with time zone information. For example:

- Date: "2023-08-05"
- Timestamp: "2023-08-05T15:30:00"

The ISO 8601 format is widely supported across different database systems and programming languages, making it less prone to ambiguity or misinterpretation. It's also less affected by regional date format settings. Using this format helps ensure consistent and correct date parsing regardless of the environment.

It's important to note that using the ISO 8601 format may still require proper handling and conversion in your code to ensure that the passed string is correctly interpreted as a date or timestamp by the database system you are using.

Question 53

How do you suppress rows affected messages when executing an insert statement in SQL Server?

In SQL Server, you can suppress the "rows affected" messages when executing an **INSERT** statement by using the **SET NOCOUNT ON** statement before your **INSERT** statement. This prevents SQL Server from sending the informational message indicating the number of rows affected by the statement.

Here's an example of how to do it:

```
SET NOCOUNT ON;

-- Your INSERT statement here
INSERT INTO YourTable (Column1, Column2) VALUES (Value1, Value2);

-- Restoring the default behavior
SET NOCOUNT OFF;
```

By setting **NOCOUNT** to **ON**, you will suppress the "X rows affected" message for the current session, making the output cleaner, especially when you are performing bulk inserts or other operations where you don't need the row count information. Remember to set **NOCOUNT** back to **OFF** afterward to restore the default behavior.

Note that this technique is specific to SQL Server. Other database systems may have different methods or settings to achieve similar results.

Question 54

Difference between ANSI-89 and ANSI-92 syntax of writing SQL Join?

The ANSI-89 **syntax uses the WHERE clause to specify join conditions,** often resulting in less readable and harder-to-maintain code. It lacks explicit JOIN keywords, leading to confusion between filtering and joining. In contrast, the ANSI-92 (or SQL-92) syntax employs explicit JOIN keywords (INNER, LEFT, RIGHT, FULL), separating join conditions from filtering conditions, enhancing code clarity and maintainability. ANSI-92 supports more complex joins, reducing ambiguity and improving query optimization. It's the recommended choice for modern SQL queries due to its structured and versatile approach to joining tables.

Question 55

Differences between IN and EXISTS (and NOT IN, and NOT EXISTS) in SQL?

IN and **EXISTS** are SQL operators that are used to filter and compare values in different ways. Similarly, **NOT IN** and **NOT EXISTS** are used for negating those comparisons. Let's explore the differences between them:

1. **IN Operator:** The **IN** operator is used to compare a value with a set of values or a subquery and returns true if the value matches any value in the set. Example:

```
SELECT * FROM employees WHERE department_id IN (101, 102, 103);
```

This query retrieves all employees from the departments with IDs 101, 102, or 103.

1. **EXISTS Operator:** The **EXISTS** operator is used to check for the existence of rows in a subquery and returns true if the subquery returns any result. Example:

```
SELECT *
FROM orders
WHERE EXISTS (
    SELECT 1
    FROM customers
    WHERE customers.customer_id = orders.customer_id
);
```

This query retrieves all orders where there is a corresponding customer in the customers table.

1. **NOT IN Operator:** The **NOT IN** operator is used to compare a value with a set of values or a subquery and returns true if the value does not match any value in the set.

Example:

```
SELECT * FROM students WHERE age NOT IN (18, 19, 20);
```

82

This query retrieves all students whose age is not 18, 19, or 20.

1. **NOT EXISTS Operator:** The **NOT EXISTS** operator is used to check for the absence of rows in a subquery and returns true if the subquery does not return any result. Example:

```
SELECT *
FROM products
WHERE NOT EXISTS (
    SELECT 1
    FROM orders
    WHERE orders.product_id = products.product_id
);
```

This query retrieves all products that have not been ordered.

Key Differences:

- **IN** and **NOT IN** compare values directly, while **EXISTS** and **NOT EXISTS** are used for existence checks based on subqueries.
- **IN** and **NOT IN** are typically used for comparing values from a list, while **EXISTS** and **NOT EXISTS** are often used for correlated subqueries (subqueries that reference columns from the outer query).
- **EXISTS** and **NOT EXISTS** are usually more efficient for checking existence compared to **IN** and **NOT IN** because they stop processing once a match is found.

In summary, **IN** and **NOT IN** are used to compare values against a list of values, whereas **EXISTS** and **NOT EXISTS** are used for checking the existence of rows based on the result of a subquery. The choice between them depends on the specific scenario and the desired outcome.

That's all on this list of **frequently asked database and SQL interview questions**. This is like a warm up for the topic-wise questions we are going to cover but if you are in hurry, you can complete this chapter and get ready for your interview in quick time.

We have also covered a lot of SQL Server questions in this list and some questions from Oracle Database but most of the questions are applicable to all the databases including MySQL. As I said, you can use this list to quickly revise the essential SQL and Database concepts before you go for the interview.

CHAPTER 2

SQL JOIN

In the world of relational databases, the ability to combine data from multiple tables is a fundamental and powerful feature. SQL Joins allow you to merge information from two or more tables based on common columns, enabling you to create a unified view of your data and extract meaningful insights.

Whether you are an aspiring data analyst or a seasoned database administrator, understanding SQL Joins is essential for querying complex datasets efficiently and effectively.

In this chapter, we will explore the concept of SQL Joins and delve into the various types of joins, preparing you to confidently tackle SQL Join-related interview questions. By the end of this chapter, you will have a comprehensive understanding of the intricacies involved in connecting tables, optimizing joins, and combining data seamlessly.

Important Topics to Prepare on Joins:

1. **Inner Join**: Understanding the most common type of join, the Inner Join, and how it returns only the rows that have matching values in both tables. Learn how to write inner join queries using the **JOIN** keyword or the explicit **INNER JOIN** syntax.

2. **Left Join (Left Outer Join)**: Exploring the Left Join, which returns all the rows from the left table and the matching rows from the right table. If there are no matches in the

85

right table, NULL values are returned. Learn how to perform left joins using the **LEFT JOIN** keyword.

3. **Right Join (Right Outer Join)**: Understanding the Right Join, which is the reverse of the Left Join, returning all rows from the right table and matching rows from the left table. If there are no matches in the left table, NULL values are returned. Master the usage of **RIGHT JOIN** to fetch data accordingly.

4. **Full Join (Full Outer Join)**: Exploring the Full Join, which returns all rows when there is a match in either the left or right table. If there are no matches in both tables, NULL values are returned. Learn how to perform Full Joins using **FULL JOIN** or combining Left and Right Joins.

5. **Cross Join (Cartesian Join)**: Understanding the Cross Join, a join that returns the Cartesian product of both tables, combining every row from the first table with every row from the second table. Master the usage of **CROSS JOIN** and its potential implications on query performance.

6. **Self Join**: Delving into the Self Join, a special case where a table is joined with itself, typically to compare records within the same table. Understand the syntax and scenarios where self joins are useful.

7. **Joining Multiple Tables**: Learning how to join more than two tables in a single query to build complex relationships and retrieve data from interconnected datasets. Understand the order of joins and the importance of parentheses in multiple join queries.

8. **Using Aliases**: Discovering the usage of table aliases to simplify query syntax and improve readability, especially when joining multiple tables or when a table is used more than once in a query.

9. **Using Join Conditions**: Mastering the art of specifying join conditions using the **ON** clause or **USING** clause (for equi-

joins). Learn how to handle complex join conditions and troubleshoot common join errors.

10. **Nested Joins**: Understanding nested joins and their role in optimizing query performance. Explore the importance of indexing and its impact on join efficiency.

11. **Anti-Join and Semi-Join**: Introducing the concepts of Anti-Join and Semi-Join, which are used to find records that do not match or partially match between two tables, respectively.

12. **Non-Equi Join**: Exploring Non-Equi Joins, where join conditions use operators other than equality, such as greater than or less than.

13. **Performance Considerations**: Understanding the importance of choosing the right join type to optimize query performance, considering the size of the tables and the data distribution.

14. **NULL Handling**: Learning how to handle NULL values during joins, including strategies to deal with NULLs in joined columns.

15. **Applying Joins in Real-World Scenarios**: Analyzing real-world examples where SQL Joins are crucial for combining data from multiple tables to answer complex business questions.

SQL Joins are a vital tool in the arsenal of any SQL professional. Whether you're seeking to consolidate data, perform data analysis, or generate meaningful reports, understanding the various types of joins and their appropriate use-cases is indispensable. By mastering SQL Joins, you will become adept at navigating through intricate database relationships and enhancing your problem-solving abilities in SQL.

Let's embark on this journey into the world of SQL Joins, empowering you to build seamless connections between tables and unlock the true potential of your data!

Below are 30 frequently asked SQL questions based upon Joins along with their answers:

Question 1

What is the difference between INNER JOIN and LEFT JOIN in SQL?

INNER JOIN returns only the rows with matching values in both tables, while LEFT JOIN returns all rows from the left table and the matching rows from the right table. If there are no matches in the right table for a left join, NULL values are returned.

Question 2

How do you perform a simple INNER JOIN between two tables in SQL?

You can use the **JOIN** keyword or the **INNER JOIN** keyword followed by the **ON** clause specifying the join condition.

For example:

```
SELECT * FROM table1
JOIN table2
ON table1.column_name = table2.column_name;
```

Question 3

Explain the usage of RIGHT JOIN with an example.

RIGHT JOIN returns all rows from the right table and the matching rows from the left table. If there are no matches in the left table, NULL values are returned.

For example:

```
SELECT * FROM employees
RIGHT JOIN departments
ON employees.department_id = departments.department_id;
```

Question 4

How can you perform a FULL JOIN to retrieve all rows from two tables, even when there are no matches?

You can use the **FULL JOIN** or combine the **LEFT JOIN** and **RIGHT JOIN** using the **UNION** operator.

For example:

```sql
SELECT * FROM table1
FULL JOIN table2
ON table1.column_name = table2.column_name;
```

Question 5

What is a SELF JOIN, and in what scenarios is it useful?

A SELF JOIN is a join where a table is joined with itself. It is useful in scenarios where you need to compare records within the same table, such as finding employees who share the same manager.

Question 6

How do you perform a SELF JOIN in SQL?

You can use table aliases to distinguish between the two instances of the same table.

For example:

```sql
SELECT e1.employee_id, e1.name AS employee_name, e2.name
AS manager_name
FROM employees e1
JOIN employees e2
ON e1.manager_id = e2.employee_id;
```

Question 7

What is the result of a CROSS JOIN?

A CROSS JOIN (also known as a Cartesian Join) returns the Cartesian product of both tables, combining every row from the first table with every row from the second table.

Question 8

How do you perform a CROSS JOIN in SQL?

You can use the **CROSS JOIN** keyword to perform a cross join.

<u>For example:</u>

```
SELECT * FROM table1 CROSS JOIN table2;
```

Question 9

Explain the concept of Non-Equi Join.

A Non-Equi Join uses join conditions other than equality. For example, using greater than or less than operators to compare values between tables.

Question 10

How do you handle NULL values during joins?

To handle NULL values during joins, you can use the **IS NULL** or **IS NOT NULL** condition in the **WHERE** clause or coalesce NULL values using the **COALESCE** function.

Question 11

What is the difference between an INNER JOIN and an equi-join?

An INNER JOIN is a type of equi-join, which means the join condition uses the equality operator (=) to match values between tables.

Question 12

How can you retrieve records from the left table that do not have corresponding matches in the right table?

You can use a LEFT JOIN and specify a condition in the **WHERE** clause to filter out rows where the right table's columns are NULL.

```
SELECT * FROM table1
LEFT JOIN table2
ON table1.column_name = table2.column_name
WHERE table2.column_name IS NULL;
```

Question 13

What is the difference between a LEFT JOIN and a RIGHT JOIN?

The difference lies in the order of tables in the join. LEFT JOIN returns all rows from the left table and matching rows from the right table, while RIGHT JOIN returns all rows from the right table and matching rows from the left table.

Question 14

How do you perform a multi-table join in SQL?

You can perform a multi-table join by chaining multiple JOIN clauses together or using parentheses to group joins.

For example:

```
SELECT * FROM table1
JOIN table2 ON table1.column_name = table2.column_name
JOIN table3 ON table2.column_name = table3.column_name;
-- OR SELECT * FROM (table1 JOIN table2 ON
table1.column_name = table2.column_name) JOIN table3 ON
table2.column_name = table3.column_name;
```

Question 15

How can you find records with no matching entries in either of the two joined tables?

You can use a FULL JOIN and specify a condition in the WHERE clause to filter out rows where either the left or right table's columns are NULL.

<u>For example:</u>

```
SELECT * FROM table1
FULL JOIN table2 ON table1.column_name =
table2.column_name
WHERE table1.column_name IS NULL OR table2.column_name IS
NULL;
```

Question 16

When should you use an INNER JOIN over a LEFT JOIN or RIGHT JOIN?

Use an INNER JOIN when you want to retrieve only the rows that have matching values in both tables. Use LEFT JOIN when you want all rows from the left table and matching rows from the right table. Use RIGHT JOIN when you want all rows from the right table and matching rows from the left table.

Question 17

How can you find records with matching values in one table but not in another?

You can use a LEFT JOIN and specify a condition in the **WHERE** clause to filter out rows where the right table's columns are NULL.

<u>For example:</u>

```
SELECT * FROM table1
LEFT JOIN table2 ON table1.column_name =
table2.column_name
WHERE table2.column_name IS NULL;
```

Question 18

What are the key differences between a FULL JOIN and a UNION?

FULL JOIN combines data from both tables, retaining non-matching rows with NULLs, while UNION combines the result sets of two or more SELECT queries, removing duplicate rows.

Question 19

How do you combine results from multiple queries without using a join?

You can use the UNION operator to combine results from multiple SELECT queries.

For example:

```
SELECT column_name FROM table1
UNION
SELECT column_name FROM table2;
```

Question 20

What is the difference between a self join and a regular join?

A self join is a join where a table is joined with itself, while a regular join is a join between two different tables. Self joins are useful when comparing records within the same table.

Question 21

How can you find the top N employees based on their salary using joins?

You can use the **ORDER BY** clause in combination with the **LIMIT** or **TOP** clause (depending on the database system) to find the top N employees based on their salary.

For example, in MySQL or PostgreSQL:

```
SELECT employee_id, name, salary
FROM employees
ORDER BY salary DESC LIMIT N;
```

In SQL Server:

```
SELECT TOP N employee_id, name, salary
FROM employees
ORDER BY salary DESC;
```

Question 22

How can you find employees who have the same manager using a self join?

You can use a self join on the **manager_id** column to find employees who share the same manager.

For example:

```
SELECT e1.employee_id, e1.name AS employee_name, e2.name
AS manager_name
FROM employees e1
JOIN employees e2 ON e1.manager_id = e2.manager_id
WHERE e1.employee_id <> e2.employee_id;
```

Question 23

What is the purpose of using table aliases in SQL joins?

Table aliases provide a shorthand notation for table names, improving query readability and reducing the amount of typing. They are especially useful when dealing with self joins or joining multiple tables.

Question 24

How can you join three or more tables in a single query?

You can use multiple JOIN clauses to join three or more tables together.

For example:

```
SELECT * FROM table1
JOIN table2 ON table1.column_name = table2.column_name
JOIN table3 ON table2.column_name = table3.column_name;
```

Question 25

Explain how you can perform a LEFT JOIN between two tables and keep only the rows that do not match.

To perform a LEFT JOIN and keep only the rows with no match, you can specify a condition in the **WHERE** clause that checks for NULL values in the right table's columns.

For example:

```
SELECT * FROM table1
LEFT JOIN table2 ON table1.column_name =
table2.column_name
WHERE table2.column_name IS NULL;
```

Question 26

Can you use a JOIN without specifying a join condition? If yes, what will be the result?

Yes, you can use a CROSS JOIN (Cartesian Join) without specifying a join condition. The result will be a combination of every row from the first table with every row from the second table, resulting in a large result set.

Question 27

What is the benefit of using an equi-join over a non-equi join?

Equi-joins are more straightforward and easier to read than non-equi joins. Additionally, equi-joins are often more efficient and can take advantage of indexes.

Question 28

How do you perform a LEFT JOIN between two tables and include all rows from the left table, even if there are multiple matches in the right table?

To include all rows from the left table, even with multiple matches in the right table, you can use the **GROUP BY** clause along with aggregate functions like **GROUP_CONCAT()** (MySQL) or **STRING_AGG()** (PostgreSQL).

For example:

```
SELECT t1.column_name, GROUP_CONCAT(t2.column_name) AS
matching_values
FROM table1 t1
LEFT JOIN table2 t2 ON t1.column_name = t2.column_name
GROUP BY t1.column_name;
```

Question 29

How do you perform an anti-join (retrieve records that exist in one table but not in another)?

You can perform an anti-join by using a LEFT JOIN and checking for NULL values in the right table's columns in the **WHERE** clause.

For example:

```
SELECT * FROM table1
LEFT JOIN table2 ON table1.column_name =
table2.column_name
WHERE table2.column_name IS NULL;
```

Question 30

How can you find the average salary of employees in each department using SQL joins?

You can use a combination of the **AVG()** aggregate function and a JOIN to calculate the average salary of employees in each department.

For example:

```
SELECT d.department_id, d.department_name, AVG(e.salary)
AS avg_salary
FROM departments d
JOIN employees e ON d.department_id = e.department_id
GROUP BY d.department_id, d.department_name;
```

These 30 SQL Join questions and their corresponding answers cover a wide range of scenarios and concepts related to SQL Joins. Practicing these questions will enhance your understanding of

SQL joins, allowing you to confidently handle interview questions and real-world data manipulation challenges.

CHAPTER 3

SQL QUERIES

Every programming job interview has at least one or two questions that require you to write SQL queries for a given requirement and many developers struggle there. It's easy to answer theoretical questions like what is the difference between clustered and non-clustered index (see) or what is the difference between correlated and non-correlated subqueries (see), but when it comes time to actually write SQL queries to solve problems, it's not that easy, especially if you haven't done your homework and practice.

In order to learn fast, start with a small table with a few columns which include data types like number, date, and String, which have fewer number data so that you can quickly understand and expect what should be output. Includes some NULL, empty, and out of bound values to really test your queries.

Considering all these together today I am going to share SQL script to create a sample table to practice writing SQL queries for interviews. In this article, you will find an SQL script to create a table and populate it with sample data and then write SQL queries to solve some common problems from Interviews.

SQL Script to create a table and Populate data

In this section, we'll see our SQL script for creating and populating the sample table required for running SQL queries. I have chosen Employee and Department table to teach you how to write SQL queries because it is one of the most popular SQL query

98

examples and most of the developers, students, and technical guys are familiar with this scheme.

This is also the example many of you have used in your academics so it's quite easy to understand and correlate. Remember, understanding schema and data is very important not only to write correct SQL queries but also to verify that your SQL query is correct by looking at the output.

The SQL queries are written for Microsoft SQL Server database and tested on the same, but you can easily run on Oracle, MySQL, or any other database of your choice by removing T-SQL code e.g. the one which checks if a table already exists, and then drop and re-create it.

Most of the code is standard ANSI SQL, hence it will run as it is on any other database. If you still face any problems then you can also check this guide to migrate SQL Server queries to Oracle.

SQL scripts to create tables

```
USE Test
GO
-- drop Employee table if already exists
IF OBJECT_ID('dbo.Employee', 'U') IS NOT NULL
BEGIN
   PRINT 'Employee Table Exists, dropping it
now'
DROP TABLE Employee;
END
-- drop Department table if already exists
IF OBJECT_ID('dbo.Department', 'U') IS NOT
NULL
BEGIN
   PRINT 'Department Table Exists, dropping it
now'
DROP TABLE Department;
END
```

```sql
-- create table ddl statments
CREATE TABLE Employee(emp_id INTEGER PRIMARY
KEY, dept_id INTEGER,
mngr_id INTEGER, emp_name VARCHAR(20), salary
INTEGER);
CREATE TABLE Department(dept_id INTEGER
PRIMARY KEY, dept_name VARCHAR(20));
-- alter table to add foreign keys
ALTER TABLE Employee ADD FOREIGN KEY (mngr_id)
REFERENCES Employee(emp_id);
ALTER TABLE Employee ADD FOREIGN KEY (dept_id)
REFERENCES Department(dept_id);
-- populating department table with sample
data
INSERT INTO Department (dept_id, dept_name)
VALUES
(1, 'Finance'),
(2, 'Legal'),
(3, 'IT'),
(4, 'Admin'),
(5, 'Empty Department');
-- populating employee table with sample data
INSERT INTO Employee(emp_id, dept_id, mngr_id,
emp_name, salary)
VALUES( 1, 1, 1, 'CEO', 100),
( 2, 3, 1, 'CTO', 95),
( 3, 2, 1, 'CFO', 100),
( 4, 3, 2, 'Java Developer', 90),
( 5, 3, 2, 'DBA', 90),
( 6, 4, 1, 'Adm 1', 20),
( 7, 4, 1, 'Adm 2', 110),
( 8, 3, 2, 'Web Developer', 50),
( 9, 3, 1, 'Middleware', 60),
( 10, 2, 3, 'Legal 1', 110),
( 11, 3, 3, 'Network', 80),
( 12, 3, 1, 'UNIX', 200);
```

This query runs on the Test database, if you don't have the `Test` database in your SQL Server instance then either create it or remove the "`USE Test`" to run on any database of your choice, you can also change the name of the database and keep the "USE".

When you run this script, it will create and populate the data the first time. When you run it again, it will drop and recreate the tables again, as shown in the following output:

```
Employee Table Exists, dropping it now
Department Table Exists, dropping it now
(5 row(s) affected)
(12 row(s) affected)
```

In this script, I have followed the naming convention and tricks which I discussed earlier in my article, a better way to write SQL queries. All the keyword is on the capital case while table names and column names are in small and camel case.

This improves the readability of SQL queries by clearing highlight which ones are keywords and which ones are object names even if syntax highlight is not available.

This example shows that just following some simple SQL best practices can seriously improve the queries you write. If you are interested in learning more SQL best practices, I suggest reading SQL Anti patterns, an interesting book for both beginners and experienced programmers.

It's time to write SQL queries now. This section contains 6 SQL query Interview questions that will test many of your SQL skills like joins, grouping, and aggregating data, how you handle nulls in SQL etc. It doesn't test all skills e.g. correlated subqueries, but you can take a look at questions like how to find Nth highest salary of employees to learn that.

This section contains 6 problems for which you need to write SQL queries, the solution is provided in the next section but I suggest you try to solve these problems first before looking at the solution.

Question 1

Can you write an SQL query to show Employee (names) who have a bigger salary than their manager?

In this problem, you need to compare employees' salaries to their manager's salary. To achieve this, you need two instances of the same table. Also in order to find a Manager you need to compare employee id with manager id, this is achieved by using the self-join in SQL, where two instances of the same table are compared.

```
-- Employees (names) who have a bigger salary than their
manager
SELECT a.emp_name FROM Employee a JOIN Employee b
ON a.mngr_id = b.emp_id
WHERE a.salary > b.salary;
```

Question 2

Write an SQL query to find Employees who have the biggest salary in their Department?

This is a little bit complex problem to solve, you first need to find the maximum salary of each department, but the department doesn't have the salary, it is the employee who has the salary. So we need to create a virtual table where we should have both department and salary.

This can be achieved by joining both Employee and Department table on `dept_id` and then using `GROUP by` clause to group salary on `dept_id`. Now, someone can question why we didn't

Since we need to print the name of the employee who has the highest salary, we need to compare each employee's salary with the department's highest salary which we have just calculated. This can be done by keeping the result of the previous query in a temp table and then joining it again with the Employee table.

```
-- Employees who have the biggest salary in their Department
SELECT a.emp_name, a.dept_id
FROM Employee a JOIN
(SELECT a.dept_id, MAX(salary) as max_salary
```

```
FROM Employee a JOIN Department b ON a.dept_id = b.dept_id
GROUP BY a.dept_id) b
ON a.salary = b.max_salary AND a.dept_id = b.dept_id;
```

Question 3

Write an SQL query to list Departments that have less than 3 people in it?

This is a rather simple SQL query interview question to solve.

You just need to know how to use the COUNT() function and GROUP BY clause.

```
-- Departments that have less than 3 people in it
SELECT dept_id, COUNT(emp_name) as 'Number of Employee'
FROM Employee
GROUP BY dept_id
HAVING COUNT(emp_name) < 3;
```

Question 4

Write an SQL query to show all Departments along with the number of people there?

This is a tricky problem, candidates often use inner join to solve the problem, leaving out empty departments.

```
-- All Department along with the number of people there
SELECT b.dept_name, COUNT(a.dept_id) as 'Number of Employee'
FROM Employee a FULL OUTER JOIN Department b ON
a.dept_id=b.dept_id
GROUP BY b.dept_name;
```

Question 5

Can you write an SQL query to show all Employees that don't have a manager in the same department?

This is similar to the first SQL query interview question, where we have used self-join to solve the problem. There we compared the salary of employee and here we have compared their department.

```
-- Employees that don't have a manager in the same
department
SELECT a.emp_name FROM Employee a JOIN Employee b
ON a.mngr_id = b.emp_id
WHERE a.dept_id != b.dept_id;
```

Question 6

Can you write SQL query to list all Departments along with the total salary there?

This problem is similar to the 4th question in this list. Here also you need to use OUTER JOIN instead of INNER join to include empty departments which should have no salaries.

```
-- All Department along with the total salary
there
SELECT b.dept_name, SUM(a.salary) as 'Total
Salary'
FROM Employee a FULL OUTER JOIN Department b
ON a.dept_id = b.dept_id
GROUP BY b.dept_name;
```

Question 7

How do you find the second highest salary in the employee table?

There are many ways to find the second highest salary in the employee table, e.g. you can either use the co-related subquery, or you can use a ranking function like row_number() and rank().

The question can be even trickier by adding duplicates, e.g. two employees with the same salary. In that case, you can choose between the ranking function to satisfy the requirement.

I have already written a detailed blog post about this topic, please see here for a couple of examples of finding the second highest salary in the employee table.

Question 8

How do you find the duplicate rows in a table?

Again, like the previous question, there are several ways to find the duplicate rows in a table, e.g. you can use a ranking function like `row_number` which assign row number depending upon the value you ask, and for the same values as in the case of duplicate rows, the row number will be same.

You can also the group by clause to detect duplicates e.g.

```
select emp_name, count(*) from employee
group by emp_name having count(*) > 1
```

This one of the classic ways to find the duplicate rows in a table, and it will work in almost all databases like Oracle, SQL Server, or MySQL.

Question 9

How do you copy all rows of a table using SQL query?(solution)

Question 10

How do you remove the duplicate rows from the table?

This is the follow-up previous question and much tougher than the previous one, especially if you are not familiar with the ranking functions like `row_number`.

If you only know about the GROUP BY clause, then you will struggle to remove duplicate rows because if you remove by emp_id, both rows will be removed. Here you must use the `row_number()` function, the duplicate rows will have `row number > 1` like

```
select emp_name, row_number() over (order by
emp_name desc) row_number
from Employee
```

This will print something like below.

John 1
Heroku 1
David 1
David 2

Here second David is duplicate, and you can easily remove it by giving conditions like `delete from table where row_number> 1`.

10. How do you join more than two tables in SQL query? (solution)

Question 11

How to find 2nd highest salary without using a co-related subquery? (solution)

Question 12

There exists an Order table and a Customer table, find all Customers who have never ordered (solution)

Don't scroll down to look at the solution until you try solving all the problems by yourself. Some of the questions are tricky, so please pay special attention to them. It's not a real interview you can take your time because all the hard work your mind will put now to find answers by its own will always remain there and that's the real learning you will get by doing this exercise.

CHAPTER 4

Indexes

A good understanding of Index is very important for any programmer working with database and SQL. It doesn't matter whether you are working as DBA or Application developer, working in Oracle, MySQL, or Microsoft SQL Server or any other database, you must have good understanding of how index works in general.

You should know different types of index and their pros and cons, how your database or Query engine chooses indexes and the **impact of table scan, index scan, and index seek**. You should also be able to build upon your knowledge to optimize your SQL queries as well as troubleshoot a production issue involving long running queries or poor performing queries. This is also a great skill for experience developers with 5 to 6 years of experience under his belt.

Since many programmers just have shallow understating of index, they began to show gaps when they face index based question on SQL Job interviews. I have taken many interviews and I am surprise that many programmer doesn't even know what is index seek and index scan and which one is faster? They are not even able to tell whether order of columns matter in a composite index or not etc?

These are very common question and if you have work in SQL or database, you might have faced those situations already.

In this article, I have compiled such question to bring them together and give them a nice overview. To keep the article short and simple, I haven't gone into too much detail but I have pointed resource to learn more if you are curious about it.

Here is my collection of some of the most common, frequently asked questions on database index.

These questions will help you to refresh your knowledge of how index work in general, barring the database differences. Btw, this list is by no means complete and if you have any good index based question then feel free to share with us.

Question 1

What is index in database?

An index is a object in database which help you to retrieve data faster. Similar to index pages of book, index are stored in separate place than data and they point to the data. Though it's not mandatory to have an index in a table, you often need index for faster retrieval of data using SELECT queries. You can create index on a column or a set of columns in a given table. The SQL clause CREATE INDEX is used to create index in a table.

Question 2

What are different types of index in Oracle or SQL Server?

There are mainly two types of indices in any database, clustered and non-clustered, but if you want to divide on number of columns then you can also say that you have a index which is based uopn just one column and then you have a composite index which is based upon a set of columns.

Question 3

How does index work?

When you create an index, there are arranged in a tree structure, so that you can navigate them in logN time. A data structure like B-Tree is used to store index but that may vary depending upon the database. Each node in index tree reference to other node and nodes at the leaf contains pointer to actual data. When you fire a SELECT query to retrieve some data, SQL query engine uses this tree to retrieve selective data. Whenever you add or remove data, this index tree is re-arranged.

Question 4

What is index scan?

When you try to retrieve data from a table which has index but you didn't provide any condition using WHERE clause then it uses index scan to search for rows in index pages. For example, if you want all employees from an employee table e.g.

```
select * from Organization.dbo.Employee;
```

Then it can use index-scan if you have a clustered index on Employee e.g. on EmployeeId. It's generally faster than table scan but slower than index seek.

Question 5

What is index seek?

The index seek is faster than index-scan because instead of scanning through all index, you directly retrieve data using pointer stored in index. This is actually the fastest way to retrieve data in a large table. This works when you have to retrieve 10 to 20% of data e.g. by specifying conditions in WHERE clause. For example, following query will use index seek, if you have an index on EmployeeId

```
select * from Organization.dbo.Empoloyee where
EmployeeId=2
```

You can even see the actual Execution Plan in Microsoft SQL Server Management Studio by pressing Ctrl + A and then running the queries as shown below:

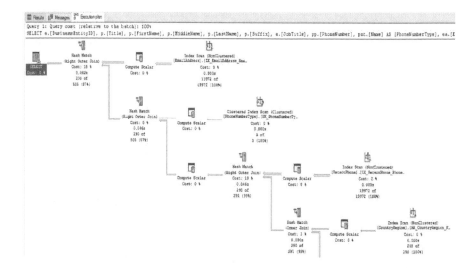

Question 6

What is difference between index scan and index seek in database?

The key difference between index scan and index seek is that seek is faster than index scan. Former is generally used when you retrieve 90% to 100% data e.g. queries without WHERE clause, while index seek is used when you selectively retrieve data e.g. by specifying conditions using WHERE or HAVING clause.

Question 7

What is difference between table scan and index scan?

There are two main ways to retrieve data from a table e.g. by using table scan or by using index. If your table is small then table scan is probably the fastest way but its in-efficient for a large table because you have to perform a lot of IO.

In a **table scan**, SQL query engine, searches all records to find the matching rows, while in index-scan it searches through index pages. If you don't have index in your table then table scan is used, but if you have clustered index then it is used even when you don't specify any condition in WHERE clause.

For example, `select * from Books` will use table scan if there is clustered index in table but will use index-scan if there is a clustered index in the table.

Question 8

What is difference between Clustered and Non-Clustered index in a table?

There are two types of indexes in a table, clustered and non-clustered. The Clustered index specifies the actual physical ordering of record in disk e.g. if you have a Book table then you can arrange them using title or ISBN number, if you create clustered index on title then they will be arranged and stored in disk in that order.

On the other hand, non-clustered index create an alternative index tree to facilitate faster retrieval of data. Since Clustered index define physical ordering, there can only be one clustered index in a table but you can have as many non-clustered index as you want.

Here is a nice diagram which clearly shows the difference between clustered and non-clustered or secondary indices in SQL:

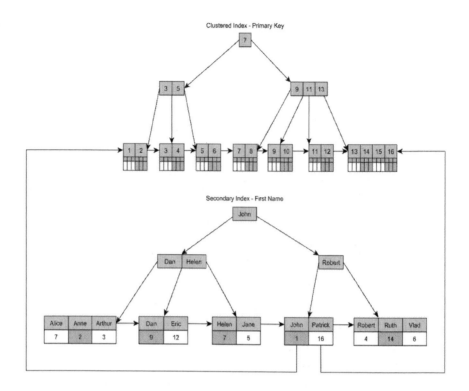

Question 9

I have a table which has clustered index on column 1, can I create another clustered index on column 2?

No, you can only have one clustered index per table, so you cannot create second one, it's not allowed.

Question 10

What is composite index in SQL?

An index may contain one or multiple columns. If a index contains multiple columns then it is known as composite index. For example,

```
-- Create a non-clustered index on a table or view
CREATE INDEX index1 ON table1 (col1);
is normal index and this one is a composite index:
-- Create a non-clustered index with a unique constraint
-- on 3 columns and specify the sort order for each
column
```

```
CREATE UNIQUE INDEX i1 ON t1 (col1 DESC, col2 ASC, col3
DESC);
```

This index is based upon three column col1, col2, and col3.

Question 11

Does the order of columns matter in a composite index?

Yes, the order of columns matters in a composite index. For example, if you have both firstname and lastname column in table and you create index on (firstname, lastname) then it can also be used in queries when you specify just one column, for example:

```
select * from Employee where firstname = 'John';
```

This query will use your composite index but following query will not use it because the mandatory column firstname is not available:

```
select * from Employee where lastname = 'kohli'
```

Hence, *order of columns matters in composite index.*

Question 12

What is the disadvantage of having many indices in a table?

Even though, index make data retrieval fast, especially in large table, you should be careful with so many index. Since index are re-arrange on every insert, update, and delete operation, there is a cost associated with them. If you execute more insert, update, and delete query than select then they will be slower because the time it will take to re-arrange all those index tree.

Index data structure also take space in your database, so if you have multiple index tree then obviously more space will be needed.

That's all about some of the **frequently asked SQL and database interview questions based upon Index.** As I said, it's very important for every programmer working with database and SQL to have a good understanding of index because it directly affects the performance of your application. A person with good knowledge of index not only write faster SQL queries but also quickly to diagnose any performance issue with their SQL queries.

We can't depend upon Database administrator or DBAs for everything, hence I advise every application developer to learn more about how index working their respective database and fill the gaps in their knowledge. You can also checkout following resources to improve you understanding of indexes in major databases like Oracle, MySQL, and Microsoft SQL Server.

CHAPTER 5

GROUP BY

THE GROUP BY clause in SQL is another important command to master for any programmer. We often use the GROUP BY command along with a select clause for reporting purposes, since the GROUP BY clause is mainly used to group related data together it's one of the most important SQL commands for reporting purposes.

Many queries that require the use of aggregate function like sum(), avg(), or count() requires the grouping of data using the GROUP BY clause. SQL queries which involve GROUP BY and HAVING clauses are also a bit confusing for many programmers who don't have hands-on experience in SQL and are often used as SQL interview questions to filter.

In this article, we will see some examples of the GROUP BY clause in SQL which help you to understand where to use group by clause and how to use GROUP BY along with the SELECT clause. You will also learn some SQL rules related to the GROUP BY clause which is available in some databases particularly in MySQL as a group by extensions.

Now it's time to see the GROUP BY clause in action. The following are some examples of how you can use GROUP BY to aggregate data and then apply filtering on aggregated or grouped data by using the HAVING clause.

1. Group By clause Example 1 - Finding duplicate

One of the popular use of the GROUP BY clause is finding duplicate records in the database. Following SQL query will list employees which are duplicate in terms of salary

```
mysql> select emp_name, count(emp_name)
       from employee group by emp_name having
count(emp_name)>1;
+-----------+-----------------+
| emp_name  | count(emp_name) |
+-----------+-----------------+
| James     |               2 |
+-----------+-----------------+
1 row in set (0.00 sec)
```

This was a rather simple example of finding duplicate records in the database. If you need to decide whether an employee is duplicate or not based upon more than one field then it's important to include all those in the group by clause, otherwise, you will get an incorrect count. You can further see my article about how to find duplicate records in the database for more details.

2. Group By clause Example 2 - Calculating Sum

Another popular example of the group by clause is using an aggregate function like sum() and avg(). If you know, the GROUP BY clause in SQL allows you to perform queries like finding how much each department is paying to employees i.e. total salaries per department.

In order to write an SQL query to find the total salary per department, we need to group by the department and use sum(salary) in the select list as shown in the following SQL query :

```
mysql> select dept_id, sum(salary) as total_salary from
employee group by dept_id;
+---------+--------------+
| dept_id | total_salary |
+---------+--------------+
|       1 |         3200 |
|       2 |         2850 |
|       3 |         2200 |
```

116

```
|        4 |         2250 |
+----------+--------------+
4 rows in set (0.00 sec)
```

Then you can further filter records by using having clauses to perform queries like finding all departments whose total salary expenditure is more than 3000. Here is an SQL query for that :

```
mysql> select dept_id, sum(salary) as total_salary
        from employee group by dept_id having sum(salary)
> 3000;
+----------+--------------+
| dept_id | total_salary |
+----------+--------------+
|       1 |         3200 |
+----------+--------------+
1 row in set (0.01 sec)
```

This is your most expensive department in terms of salary. It's stood to know the useful aggregate function like count and sum.

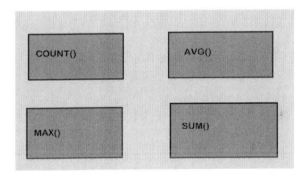

3. How to calculate average using group by clause

Similar to the previous group by clause example, instead of sum() we can also use avg() to perform queries like *finding out average salary of employees per department*. Once again we need to group by the department and this time instead of sum() aggregate function we need to use the avg() function as shown in the below query :

```
mysql> select dept_id, avg(salary) as average_salary from
employee group by dept_id;
+----------+--------------------+
| dept_id | average_salary |
```

```
+----------+---------------+
|       1 |     1066.6667 |
|       2 |     1425.0000 |
|       3 |     1100.0000 |
|       4 |      750.0000 |
+----------+---------------+
4 rows in set (0.00 sec)
```

Similarly, you can use having clause to further filter down this result set like finding a department whose average salary is below 1000. Here is an SQL query for that :

```
mysql> select dept_id, avg(salary) as average_salary
from employee group by dept_id having avg(salary) < 1000;
+----------+----------------+
| dept_id | average_salary |
+----------+----------------+
|       4 |      750.0000 |
+----------+----------------+
1 row in set (0.00 sec)
```

This is your most poorly paid department. There is no point going into that department and exploring further.

4. Group By example 4 - Counting records

Similar to aggregate function sum() and avg(), another kind of aggregate query is very popular like counting records.

One example of this kind of group by the query is *how to find the number of employees per department?*

In this case, we need to group by the department and need to use the count() aggregate function for counting employees as shown in the below SQL query :

```
mysql> select dept_id, count(emp_id) as
number_of_employees
         from employee group by dept_id;
+----------+---------------------+
| dept_id | number_of_employees |
+----------+---------------------+
|       1 |                   3 |
|       2 |                   2 |
|       3 |                   2 |
```

118

While using the count() function in SQL, it's worth noting the difference between count() and count(field) which could give different counts based upon which column on which you are counting and whether that column contains NULL or not.

Just remember count() also counts NULL values in a column. NULLs are very special in SQL and you should have a good knowledge of how to use Null and how to compare them.

5. How to use Group By clause with more than one column

In many practical cases, we use a group by clause with more than one column. While using two or three-column in the group by clause order is very important. The column which comes first on the group by clause will be grouped first and then the second column will be used to do grouping on that group. For example in the following SQL query result set is first grouped by dept_id and then each group is again grouped by emp_id.

```
mysql> select dept_id, emp_id from employee group by
dept_id, emp_id;
+---------+--------+
| dept_id | emp_id |
+---------+--------+
|       1 |    101 |
|       1 |    102 |
|       1 |    110 |
|       2 |    103 |
|       2 |    104 |
|       3 |    105 |
|       3 |    108 |
|       4 |    106 |
|       4 |    107 |
|       4 |    109 |
+---------+--------+
10 rows in set (0.00 sec)
```

Another example of using multiple columns in group by clause is finding duplicate records in the table, where you must use all

119

columns which are required to be the same for a record to be called duplicates

Important points about Group By clause in SQL

Now it's time to revise and revisit some of the important things about the GROUP BY clause in SQL statements.

1. You can not use a **non-aggregated column** name in the select list if it is not used in Group By clause. For example following SQL query is illegal and will not run because it has used a non-aggregate column emp_id in the select list which is not named in Group By clause, in this SQL query only dept_id is used in group by clause.

```
mysql> select emp_id, dept_id, max(salary)
       from employee
       groupby dept_id;
ERROR 1055 (42000): 'test.employee.emp_id' isn't
inGROUPBY
```

but MySQL database permits it by its group by extension functionality which is disabled in the above scenario by enabling ONLY_FULL_GROUP_BY SQL mode.

2. In standard SQL you cannot use a non-aggregated column name in the Having clause which is not used in group by clause, MySQL database also allows it similar to the previous group by extension. Following SQL query is invalid because we are using max_salary in having a clause that is not used in group by clause.

```
mysql> select dept_id, max(salary) as max_salary
       from employee
       groupby dept_id having max_salary > 1000;
ERROR 1463 (42000): Non-grouping field 'max_salary'is
used in HAVING clause
```

3. Another rule of using group by clause in standard SQL is that you **cannot use an alias in the HAVING clause**, the previous

SQL query is also an example of this group by rule. This is also allowed in the MySQL database.

You can disable all MySQL group by extension features by using ONLY_FULL_GROUP_BY SQL mode in MySQL. In order to change SQL mode from the MySQL command line you can use the following MySQL commands :

```
mysql> SET GLOBAL
sql_mode='STRICT_TRANS_TABLES,NO_AUTO_CREATE_USER,
          NO_ENGINE_SUBSTITUTION,ONLY_FULL_GROUP_BY';
Query OK, 0 rows affected (0.00 sec)
mysql> SELECT @@GLOBAL.sql_mode;
+-------------------------------------------------------
-------------------------------+
| @@GLOBAL.sql_mode
|
+-------------------------------------------------------
-------------------------------+
|
ONLY_FULL_GROUP_BY,STRICT_TRANS_TABLES,NO_AUTO_CREATE_USE
R,NO_ENGINE_SUBSTITUTION |
+-------------------------------------------------------
-------------------------------+
1 row in set (0.00 sec)
```

You can also set MySQL SQL mode for a single client session by using the word SESSION instead of GLOBAL as shown below :

```
mysql> SET SESSION
sql_mode='STRICT_TRANS_TABLES,NO_AUTO_CREATE_USER,
          NO_ENGINE_SUBSTITUTION,ONLY_FULL_GROUP_BY';
Query OK, 0 rows affected (0.00 sec)
mysql> SELECT @@GLOBAL.sql_mode;
+-------------------------------------------------------
-------------------------------+
| @@GLOBAL.sql_mode
|
+-------------------------------------------------------
-------------------------------+
|
ONLY_FULL_GROUP_BY,STRICT_TRANS_TABLES,NO_AUTO_CREATE_USE
R,NO_ENGINE_SUBSTITUTION |
+-------------------------------------------------------
-------------------------------+
1 row in set (0.00 sec)
```

Also just changing MySQL SQL mode to Global will not take effect in the current session until you restart a new session. In order to enable ONLY_FULL_GROUP_BY in the current MySQL session using the above query.

That's all on the GROUP BY clause example in SQL queries. We have seen where to use the GROUP BY command and How to use the GROUP BY clause to group data in SQL. As I said GROUP BY and HAVING clause is one of the must-know for any programmers as it's quite common in the SQL world and particularly important for reporting purposes.

CHAPTER 6

SQL Date and Time Interview Questions

Welcome to the SQL Date and Time Interview Questions chapter of this book! In the world of data manipulation and analysis, *understanding how to work with dates and times* is of paramount importance.

As the saying goes, "time is money," and this holds true especially in the realm of database management and querying. In today's competitive job market, employers often seek candidates with a strong grasp of SQL's date and time functions, as these skills play a crucial role in handling time-sensitive data effectively.

In this chapter, we will delve into the essential aspects of SQL date and time handling, preparing you to confidently tackle interview questions related to this critical topic.

Whether you are a seasoned SQL professional looking to refresh your knowledge or a job seeker preparing for upcoming technical interviews, this chapter will serve as a comprehensive guide to mastering date and time manipulations in SQL.

Key Topics and Concepts to Prepare:

Date and Time Data Types: Understanding the various date and time data types supported by SQL databases, such as DATE, TIME, DATETIME, TIMESTAMP, etc., and knowing when to use each type appropriately.

123

Date and Time Functions: Familiarizing yourself with the wide array of SQL functions designed to extract, manipulate, and format date and time values. Some crucial functions include DATEPART, EXTRACT, DATEADD, DATEDIFF, TO_DATE, TO_CHAR, and many more.

Date and Time Arithmetic: Learning how to perform arithmetic operations with dates and times, such as calculating the difference between two dates, adding or subtracting days, months, or years, and finding the day of the week.

Time Zones and Time Zone Conversions: Understanding the challenges of working with time zones in a globalized world and how to handle time zone conversions within SQL queries.

Date and Time Constraints: Exploring the concept of date and time constraints, including defining constraints on columns to ensure the validity and integrity of date and time data stored in a database.

Date and Time Formatting: Gaining insights into formatting date and time values for display purposes, including custom date formats and converting between different date formats.

Handling Time Intervals: Grasping the methods to manage and perform calculations with time intervals, such as finding overlapping time periods or determining the duration between two events.

Date and Time in Joins and Conditions: Understanding how to use date and time values effectively in JOIN clauses, WHERE clauses, and other conditional statements to filter and combine data accurately.

Best Practices: Learning industry best practices for working with dates and times, optimizing queries, and ensuring efficient date-related operations in SQL databases.

Whether you aspire to work as a database administrator, data analyst, or any other SQL-related role, proficiency in SQL date and time operations is an indispensable skill. So, let's dive into the world of date and time manipulation in SQL, explore its nuances, and equip ourselves with the knowledge to excel in SQL date and time interview questions.

Now, let's see a frequently asked SQL questions related to Date and Time:

Question 1

How do you find all records modified between two dates in SQL?

This is one of the tricky SQL questions. It looks simple, but when you go and write the SQL query, you will find that it's not working as expected. For example, many programmers will use the "between" SQL clause to find all the rows modified between two dates e.g.

```
select * from Orders where order_date
between '20160901' and '20160930'
```

This will work well in most cases, but if there is an order where order_date is midnight of 1st October, then it will also be picked. You can be more precise by using the logical operator, as shown below:

```
select * from Orders where order_date
>='20160901' and order_date < '20160930'
```

Question 2

How do you extract the year from a date in SQL?

You can extract the year from a date using the **YEAR()** function.

For example:

```
SELECT YEAR(date_column) FROM table_name;
```

Question 3

How can you add 3 months to a given date in SQL?

You can add 3 months to a date using the **DATEADD()** function.

For example:

```
SELECTDATEADD(MONTH, 3, date_column) FROM table_name;
```

Question 4

How do you find the number of days between two dates in SQL?

You can find the number of days between two dates using the **DATEDIFF()** function.

For example:

```
SELECT DATEDIFF(DAY, start_date, end_date) FROM table_name;
```

Question 5

Explain the difference between DATE and DATETIME data types.

DATE stores only the date without any time information, while **DATETIME** stores both the date and the time.

Question 6.

How do you convert a date to a different date format in SQL?

You can use the **CONVERT()** or **FORMAT()** function to convert a date to a different format. For example:

```
SELECT CONVERT(varchar, date_column, 105)
```

```
FROM table_name;
-- OR SELECT FORMAT(date_column, 'dd-MM-yyyy') FROM
table_name;
```

Question 7

How can you find records that fall within a specific month and year?

You can use the **MONTH()** and **YEAR()** functions in combination with the **WHERE** clause. For example:

```
SELECT * FROM table_name
WHERE MONTH(date_column) = 7 AND YEAR(date_column) =
2023;
```

Question 8

How do you handle time zone conversions in SQL?

To handle time zone conversions, you can use the **AT TIME ZONE** clause (for SQL Server) or the **AT TIME ZONE** function (for PostgreSQL).

For example:

```
SELECT date_column AT TIME ZONE 'UTC' AS
converted_date FROM table_name;
```

Question 9

Can you enforce a constraint to ensure a date column always contains future dates?

Yes, you can use a constraint with the **CHECK** keyword to enforce this.

For example:

```
ALTER TABLE table_name
ADD CONSTRAINT future_date_constraint CHECK (date_column
> GETDATE());
```

Question 10

How can you find the first and last day of the current month?

You can use the **EOMONTH()** function to find the last day and then subtract the number of days in the month minus one to find the first day.

For example:

```
SELECTDATEADD(DAY, 1, EOMONTH(GETDATE(), -1)) AS
first_day_of_month, EOMONTH(GETDATE()) AS
last_day_of_month;
```

Question 11

How do you find records with overlapping date ranges in SQL?

You can use the **BETWEEN** operator to check for overlapping date ranges.

For example:

```
SELECT * FROM table_name
WHERE start_date BETWEEN'2023-01-01'
AND'2023-12-31'
OR end_date BETWEEN'2023-01-01'AND'2023-12-31';
```

Question 12

How can you calculate the age of a person from their birthdate?

You can use the **DATEDIFF()** function to calculate the difference in years between the birthdate and the current date.

For example:

```
SELECT DATEDIFF(YEAR, birthdate, GETDATE()) AS age
FROM table_name;
```

Question 13

Explain the significance of the UNIX timestamp and how to convert it to a readable date format.

The UNIX timestamp represents the number of seconds that have elapsed since January 1, 1970 (UTC). To convert it to a readable date format, you can use the **FROM_UNIXTIME()** function (for MySQL) or the **TO_TIMESTAMP()** function (for PostgreSQL). For example:

SELECT FROM_UNIXTIME(unix_timestamp_column) AS readable_date FROM table_name; -- OR SELECT TO_TIMESTAMP(unix_timestamp_column) AS readable_date FROM table_name;

Question 14

How do you get the current date and time in SQL?

You can use the **GETDATE()** or **CURRENT_TIMESTAMP** function to get the current date and time. For example:

SELECT GETDATE() AS current_date_time; -- OR SELECT CURRENT_TIMESTAMP AS current_date_time;

Question 15

How can you convert a string to a date in SQL?

You can use the **CAST()** or **CONVERT()** functions to convert a string to a date.

For example:

```
SELECTCAST('2023-07-16'ASDATE) AS converted_date;
-- OR SELECT CONVERT(DATE, '2023-07-16') AS
converted_date;
```

Question 16

How do you find the day of the week for a given date in SQL?

You can use the **DATEPART()** function with the **dw** parameter to find the day of the week (Sunday = 1, Monday = 2, etc.). For example:

SELECT DATEPART(dw, date_column) AS day_of_week FROM table_name;

Can you explain the importance of using the **UTC_TIMESTAMP()** function when dealing with international applications?

The **UTC_TIMESTAMP()** function returns the current date and time in Coordinated Universal Time (UTC). Using UTC ensures consistency across different time zones, making it essential when dealing with international applications to avoid confusion and data inconsistencies

Question 17

How do you find the number of weekdays (excluding weekends) between two dates?

You can use a combination of **DATEDIFF()** and **DATEPART()** functions to find the number of weekdays between two dates. For example:

```
SELECT (DATEDIFF(dd, start_date, end_date) + 1)
- (DATEDIFF(wk, start_date, end_date) * 2)
- CASE
WHENDATEPART(dw, start_date) = 1
THEN1
ELSE0
END
- CASEWHENDATEPART(dw, end_date) = 7
THEN1
ELSE0
END AS weekdays_count
FROM table_name;
```

Question 18

How do you extract the time part from a DATETIME column in SQL?

You can use the **CONVERT()** function with a style parameter of 108 to extract the time part. For example:

```
SELECTCONVERT(TIME, datetime_column, 108) AS
extracted_time
FROM table_name;
```

Question 19

How can you find the records with the latest date in a table?

You can use the **MAX()** function to find the latest date in a table. For example:

```
SELECT MAX(date_column) AS latest_date
FROM table_name;
```

Question 20

Explain the concept of leap years and how you would identify if a year is a leap year in SQL.

Leap years are years with an extra day, February 29, to keep the calendar year synchronized with the astronomical year. In SQL, you can identify a leap year by checking if the year is divisible by 4, except for years divisible by 100, which are not leap years unless they are also divisible by 400. For example:

```
SELECT
CASE
    WHEN (year_column % 4 = 0
        AND year_column % 100 != 0) OR (year_column
% 400 = 0)
    THEN'Leap Year'
    ELSE'Not a Leap Year'
END
AS leap_year_status FROM table_name;
```

These **20 SQL Date and Time Interview Questions** cover a wide range of topics, from basic date and time manipulations to more advanced functions and constraints. Familiarizing yourself with these concepts and practicing their implementation will undoubtedly boost your confidence when facing date and time-related interview questions in SQL. Remember that hands-on practice with real-world scenarios will reinforce your understanding and help you excel in SQL interviews. Good luck!

CHAPTER 7

Aggregate Functions

Aggregate functions are essential tools in database management that allow you to perform calculations on sets of data and return single values as results. These functions enable you to summarize, group, and analyze data efficiently, making them invaluable for generating meaningful insights from large datasets. Common aggregate functions include SUM, COUNT, AVG, MIN, MAX, and more, each serving a specific purpose in data analysis.

In this chapter, we will explore the world of aggregate functions and delve into the key topics that form the foundation of effective data summarization and analysis. Whether you are a database professional, a data analyst, or a developer, understanding aggregate functions is crucial for gaining valuable information from databases.

Important Topics to Prepare on Aggregate Functions:

1. **Introduction to Aggregate Functions**: Understanding the concept of aggregate functions, their role in data summarization, and the benefits they offer.

2. **Common Aggregate Functions**: Familiarizing yourself with essential aggregate functions, such as SUM, COUNT, AVG, MIN, MAX, and their syntax in SQL.

3. **Grouping Data**: Learning how to use GROUP BY clauses to group data based on specific columns for aggregation.

4. **HAVING Clause**: Understanding the HAVING clause, which filters the results of the GROUP BY operation based on specific conditions.

5. **Distinct vs. All**: Differentiating between using DISTINCT and ALL keywords with aggregate functions to control duplicate values.

6. **NULL Handling**: Grasping how aggregate functions treat NULL values and the use of the COALESCE or NULLIF functions to manage NULLs.

7. **Combining Aggregate Functions**: Learning how to use multiple aggregate functions in a single query to generate comprehensive data summaries.

8. **Nested Aggregations**: Understanding the challenges and solutions when applying aggregate functions within subqueries or nested queries.

9. **Rollup and Cube**: Exploring the ROLLUP and CUBE operators for generating multiple levels of subtotal and grand total summaries.

10. **String Aggregation**: Learning techniques to concatenate strings from multiple rows using aggregate functions.

11. **Aggregates and Joins**: Analyzing the interaction of aggregate functions with different types of joins in SQL queries.

12. **Performance Considerations**: Understanding the impact of using aggregate functions on query performance and potential optimizations.

13. **Aggregates in Window Functions**: Exploring how aggregate functions are used in combination with window functions for advanced data analysis.

14. **Using GROUPING SETS**: Understanding the GROUPING SETS clause for specifying multiple grouping sets within a single query.

15. **Aggregates in Real-World Scenarios**: Discovering how aggregate functions are applied in real-world scenarios like sales analysis, financial reporting, and business intelligence.

16. **Custom Aggregate Functions**: Learning how to create custom user-defined aggregate functions in certain database systems.

17. **Aggregates in NoSQL Databases**: Exploring the usage of aggregate-like operations in NoSQL databases, where traditional aggregate functions may not be available.

18. **Aggregates and Data Visualization**: Understanding how aggregate functions are utilized in data visualization tools and dashboards.

19. **Handling Large Datasets**: Analyzing strategies to handle large datasets efficiently when using aggregate functions.

20. **Aggregates and Data Analysis Tools**: Familiarizing yourself with the integration of aggregate functions with data analysis tools like Excel and Python libraries.

Aggregate functions arc fundamental tools for data summarization and analysis in databases. By mastering the concepts and practices of aggregate functions, you can gain valuable insights from data and make informed decisions in various domains.

In the following chapters, we will delve into each of these topics, providing you with in-depth knowledge and practical insights into aggregate functions and their significance in modern database management and data analysis. Let's embark on this journey into the realm of aggregate functions and uncover their true potential in data-driven decision making!

Below are 20+ common questions on aggregate functions, along with their answers:

Question 1

What are aggregate functions in SQL, and what is their purpose?

Aggregate functions are SQL functions used to perform calculations on sets of data and return a single value as a result. Their purpose is to summarize, group, or analyze data in queries.

Question 2

List some common aggregate functions in SQL.

Common aggregate functions include SUM, COUNT, AVG, MIN, MAX, and others.

Question 3

How do you use the COUNT function to count the number of rows in a table?

To count the number of rows in a table, you can use the COUNT function with the **SELECT** statement and specify the column or use **COUNT(*)** to count all rows.

Question 4

What is the difference between the COUNT function with DISTINCT and without DISTINCT?

COUNT function with DISTINCT counts only the distinct (unique) values, while without DISTINCT, it counts all occurrences, including duplicates.

Question 5

How can you use the SUM function to calculate the total value of a specific column?

To calculate the total value of a specific column, use the SUM function with the **SELECT** statement and specify the column.

Question 6

How do you calculate the average (mean) of a column using the AVG function?

To calculate the average of a column, use the AVG function with the **SELECT** statement and specify the column.

Question 7

Explain the usage of the GROUP BY clause with aggregate functions.

The GROUP BY clause is used to group rows based on specified columns. When used with aggregate functions, it calculates aggregates for each group.

Question 8

How does the HAVING clause differ from the WHERE clause when using aggregate functions?

The WHERE clause filters individual rows before grouping, while the HAVING clause filters the result of the GROUP BY operation.

Question 9

What is the purpose of the ROLLUP operator in aggregate functions?

The ROLLUP operator is used to generate multiple levels of subtotal and grand total summaries in a single query.

Question 10

Can you use multiple aggregate functions in a single SQL query?

Yes, you can use multiple aggregate functions in a single query to generate comprehensive data summaries.

Question 11

How do you handle NULL values when using aggregate functions?

Aggregate functions generally ignore NULL values. You can use the COALESCE or NULLIF functions to manage NULLs before using aggregate functions.

Question 12

What is string aggregation, and how can you achieve it in SQL?

String aggregation involves concatenating strings from multiple rows into a single string. In SQL, you can use functions like GROUP_CONCAT (MySQL), STRING_AGG (PostgreSQL), or LISTAGG (Oracle) for this purpose.

Question 13

How do aggregate functions interact with different types of joins?

Aggregate functions can be used in combination with various types of joins (INNER JOIN, LEFT JOIN, etc.) to analyze and summarize related data.

Question 14

Can you use aggregate functions with window functions?

Yes, aggregate functions can be used in combination with window functions for advanced data analysis and ranking.

Question 15

How do you optimize the performance of queries using aggregate functions on large datasets?

To optimize performance, you can use appropriate indexes, minimize data retrieval, and ensure the use of efficient query plans.

Question 16

What is the purpose of the GROUPING SETS clause in aggregate functions?

The GROUPING SETS clause allows you to specify multiple grouping sets within a single query, enabling you to generate different levels of aggregates.

Question 17

How do you apply aggregate functions in real-world scenarios like sales analysis or financial reporting?

In sales analysis, aggregate functions can be used to calculate total revenue, average sales, and other metrics. In financial reporting, they can summarize financial data like expenses, revenue, and profits.

Question 18

How are aggregate functions used in data visualization and reporting tools?

Aggregate functions play a crucial role in data visualization tools, where they summarize data for charts, graphs, and dashboards.

Question 19

Can you create custom aggregate functions in SQL?

Some database systems allow you to create custom user-defined aggregate functions, extending the functionality beyond built-in aggregates.

Question 20

Explain how you use aggregate functions with NoSQL databases.

NoSQL databases may not support traditional aggregate functions, but they provide similar capabilities through specialized aggregation mechanisms or MapReduce paradigms.

What is the difference between count(field) and count(*) in SQL?

The only difference between count(field) and count(*) is that the former doesn't count null values while the latter does. For example, if you have an emp_name column on your table and it contains 10 valid values and 3 null values, then count(emp_name) will return 10 while count(*) will return 13 rows.

These questions cover various aspects of aggregate functions in SQL and their usage in data summarization and analysis. Preparing for these questions will help you demonstrate your proficiency in handling data using aggregate functions in database management and data analysis scenarios.

CHAPTER 8

Stored Procedure

Stored procedures are a vital component of database management systems, providing a means to encapsulate and execute a set of SQL statements as a single unit. By creating reusable stored procedures, database administrators and developers can enhance data security, simplify complex operations, improve code maintainability, and optimize database performance. Stored procedures serve as essential building blocks for various database-driven applications and play a crucial role in enhancing productivity and data integrity.

In this chapter, we will explore the realm of stored procedures and delve into the key topics that form the foundation of efficient database management. Whether you are a database professional or a developer, understanding stored procedures is essential for effective data manipulation and application development.

Important Topics to Prepare on Stored Procedures:

1. **Introduction to Stored Procedures**: Understanding the concept of stored procedures, their purpose, and the advantages they bring to database management.

2. **Creating Stored Procedures**: Exploring the syntax and process of creating stored procedures in SQL or other supported database languages.

3. **Input and Output Parameters**: Learning how to pass input parameters to stored procedures for dynamic data

processing and how to return output parameters or result sets.

4. **Stored Procedure Execution**: Understanding how to execute stored procedures using various methods, including SQL queries and application code.

5. **Procedure Variables and Local Declarations**: Grasping the usage of variables and local declarations within stored procedures for temporary data storage and manipulation.

6. **Conditional Processing**: Learning how to implement conditional logic (IF-ELSE) and iterative loops (WHILE, FOR) within stored procedures.

7. **Error Handling**: Understanding the importance of error handling in stored procedures and how to use TRY...CATCH blocks or EXCEPTION handling to manage errors gracefully.

8. **Dynamic SQL**: Exploring the use of dynamic SQL within stored procedures to generate and execute SQL statements at runtime.

9. **Common Built-In Functions**: Familiarizing yourself with common built-in functions used within stored procedures, such as string manipulation, date and time functions, and mathematical operations.

10. **Security and Permissions**: Understanding how to grant appropriate permissions for executing, altering, or dropping stored procedures.

11. **Stored Procedure Performance**: Analyzing best practices for optimizing stored procedure performance, including query optimization, parameterization, and proper indexing.

12. **Procedural vs. Declarative**: Differentiating between procedural programming (used in stored procedures) and declarative SQL statements.

13. **Dependencies and Recompilation**: Exploring how changes to underlying tables and objects impact stored procedures and how they are recompiled when necessary.

14. **Nested and Recursive Stored Procedures**: Understanding the concept of nesting stored procedures and handling recursion for advanced data processing.

15. **Stored Procedures in Transactions**: Learning how to manage stored procedures within transactions for data integrity and consistency.

16. **Debugging Stored Procedures**: Exploring techniques and tools for debugging stored procedures during development and troubleshooting.

17. **Stored Procedures vs. Functions**: Comparing stored procedures with user-defined functions and understanding their respective use cases.

18. **Stored Procedures in Application Development**: Discovering how stored procedures are integrated into application development frameworks and enhancing database interactions.

19. **Dynamic Result Sets**: Understanding how to work with stored procedures that return dynamic result sets or multiple result sets.

20. **Stored Procedures Best Practices**: Learning best practices for designing, naming, and organizing stored procedures to ensure maintainability and code reusability.

Stored procedures are a cornerstone of efficient and secure database management. By mastering the concepts and practices of stored procedures, you can streamline database operations, enhance application development, and create robust and scalable database-driven applications.

In the following chapters, we will delve into each of these topics, providing you with in-depth knowledge and practical insights into stored procedures and their significance in modern database management and application development. Let's embark on this journey into the realm of stored procedures and uncover their true potential in the world of databases!

Below are some important questions on stored procedures along with their answers for interviews:

Question 1

What is a stored procedure?

A stored procedure is a pre-compiled and reusable database object that contains a group of SQL statements. It is stored in the database and can be executed by calling its name.

Question 2

What are the advantages of using stored procedures?

Some advantages of using stored procedures include:

- Improved performance due to pre-compilation.
- Enhanced security by controlling data access through procedures.
- Simplified complex operations by encapsulating logic.
- Reduced network traffic by sending only the procedure call rather than multiple SQL statements.

Question 3

How do you create a stored procedure in SQL?

To create a stored procedure in SQL, you use the **CREATE PROCEDURE** statement, followed by the procedure name, input parameters (if any), and the SQL statements that define the procedure.

Question 4

How do you call a stored procedure from SQL or an application?

You can call a stored procedure using the **EXECUTE** or **EXEC** statement in SQL, or by invoking it from application code using the appropriate database library or framework.

Question 5

What are input and output parameters in stored procedures?

Input parameters allow you to pass values to the stored procedure when it is called. Output parameters allow the procedure to return values back to the caller.

Question 6

How do you handle errors in a stored procedure?

Errors in stored procedures can be handled using TRY...CATCH blocks (in SQL Server) or EXCEPTION blocks (in PostgreSQL and other databases) to catch and handle exceptions gracefully.

Question 7

Can a stored procedure call another stored procedure?

Yes, stored procedures can call other stored procedures, either within the same database or in different databases.

Question 8

What are the different types of parameters that a stored procedure can have?

A stored procedure can have input parameters, output parameters, and parameters that serve both as input and output (INOUT).

Question 9

How do you pass multiple values to a stored procedure as a single parameter?

To pass multiple values as a single parameter, you can use techniques like passing comma-separated values, XML, or JSON data.

Question 10

What is dynamic SQL, and when is it useful in stored procedures?

Dynamic SQL involves generating and executing SQL statements at runtime within a stored procedure. It is useful when the structure of the query needs to change dynamically based on user inputs or conditions.

Question 11

How can you improve the performance of a stored procedure?

Performance of a stored procedure can be improved by optimizing the underlying SQL queries, using appropriate indexes, and parameterizing queries to avoid SQL injection.

Question 12

How do you grant permissions to execute a stored procedure?

You can grant execution permissions to a stored procedure using the **GRANT EXECUTE** statement to specific users or roles.

Question 13

Can a stored procedure return multiple result sets?

Yes, a stored procedure can return multiple result sets, and they can be accessed one by one from the application code.

Question 14

What is the difference between a stored procedure and a user-defined function?

Stored procedures are primarily used for data manipulation and complex logic, while user-defined functions are used to return scalar values or table-valued results.

Question 15

How do you debug a stored procedure?

You can use debugging tools provided by the database management system or print debugging information to identify issues in the stored procedure code.

Question 16

What are nested stored procedures?

Nested stored procedures are procedures that call other stored procedures within their logic.

Question 17

How do you view the source code of a stored procedure?

The source code of a stored procedure can usually be viewed using system catalogs or metadata views specific to the database system.

Question 18

Can you use transactions within a stored procedure?

Yes, stored procedures can include transactions to ensure data integrity and consistency during complex operations.

Question 19

How do you drop a stored procedure?

You can drop a stored procedure using the **DROP PROCEDURE** statement.

Question 20

What are the best practices for writing efficient and maintainable stored procedures?

Some best practices include using meaningful and consistent naming conventions, modularizing procedures, handling errors, and commenting the code for clarity.

These questions cover various aspects of stored procedures and their usage in database management and application development. Preparing for these questions will help you demonstrate your understanding of stored procedures and their practical implementation in different scenarios.

CHAPTER 9

Triggers and Views

One of the important features of Spring Boot is the auto-configuration, which makes it possible

Database triggers and views are powerful features in database management systems that enhance data manipulation, simplify complex queries, and enable automation of actions based on specified events. Triggers are special stored procedures that automatically execute when specific events occur, such as insertions, updates, or deletions on a table. On the other hand, views are virtual tables created from the result of a SELECT query, allowing users to interact with the data without directly modifying the underlying tables.

In this chapter, we will explore the world of database triggers and views, uncovering their significance in data management and query optimization. Whether you are a database administrator, a data analyst, or a developer, understanding triggers and views is essential for streamlining database operations and enhancing data accessibility.

Important Topics to Prepare on Database Triggers and Views:

1. **Introduction to Triggers**: Understanding the concept of triggers, their purpose, and the different types of triggers available in database systems.

2. **Trigger Events**: Learning about various trigger events, such as INSERT, UPDATE, DELETE, and how triggers respond to these events.

3. **Creating Triggers**: Exploring the syntax and process of creating triggers in SQL.

4. **Trigger Execution Time**: Understanding the timing of trigger execution, such as BEFORE or AFTER the triggering event.

5. **Use Cases of Triggers**: Discovering real-world scenarios where triggers are useful, such as enforcing data integrity, maintaining audit trails, and implementing complex business logic.

6. **Managing Triggers**: Learning how to enable, disable, modify, or drop triggers as part of database maintenance.

7. **Benefits and Drawbacks of Triggers**: Analyzing the advantages and potential pitfalls of using triggers in database design.

8. **Introduction to Views**: Understanding the concept of views and their role in data abstraction.

9. **Creating Views**: Exploring the process of creating and managing views in SQL.

10. **Updating Through Views**: Learning how to perform data modifications through views and understanding the restrictions associated with updateable views.

11. **Materialized Views**: Differentiating between regular views and materialized views, which store the query results physically for faster data retrieval.

12. **Nested Views**: Understanding the concept of nested views, where a view is based on another view.

13. **Use Cases of Views**: Discovering real-world applications of views, such as data simplification, access control, and query optimization.

14. **Indexed Views**: Analyzing the benefits of indexed views, which improve query performance by precomputing and storing aggregated data.

15. **Security Considerations**: Exploring security considerations when using views, including permissions and data exposure.

16. **Combining Views and Joins**: Learning how to use views in combination with joins to simplify complex queries.

17. **View Maintenance**: Understanding how views impact data maintenance and updates to the underlying tables.

18. **Updatable Views and INSTEAD OF Triggers**: Exploring the concept of updatable views and how to use INSTEAD OF triggers to handle updates on non-updatable views.

19. **Recursion in Views**: Understanding the use of recursive views to work with hierarchical data structures.

20. **Views vs. Materialized Views**: Comparing regular views and materialized views in terms of performance and data consistency.

Database triggers and views are valuable tools that facilitate data management, simplify query execution, and automate tasks within a database system. By mastering the concepts and practices of triggers and views, you can optimize database performance, enhance data accessibility, and ensure data integrity in various database applications.

In the following sections, we will delve into each of these topics, providing you with comprehensive knowledge and practical insights into database triggers and views. Let's embark on this journey into the realm of triggers and views and understand their significance in modern database management!

Below are 20+ common questions on database triggers and views, along with their answers:

Question 1

What is a database trigger, and what events can trigger its execution?

A database trigger is a special type of stored procedure that automatically executes in response to specific events, such as INSERT, UPDATE, or DELETE operations on a table.

Question 2

How do you create a trigger in SQL?

To create a trigger in SQL, you use the **CREATE TRIGGER** statement, specifying the trigger name, the trigger timing (BEFORE or AFTER), the triggering event (INSERT, UPDATE, or DELETE), and the action to be performed in response to the event.

Question 3

What is the difference between a BEFORE trigger and an AFTER trigger?

A BEFORE trigger executes before the triggering event, allowing you to modify data before it is actually inserted, updated, or deleted. An AFTER trigger executes after the triggering event, acting on the data after the change has taken place.

Question 4

In what scenarios are triggers commonly used?

Triggers are commonly used to enforce data integrity constraints, maintain audit trails, implement complex business logic, and propagate changes to related tables.

Question 5

How can you enable or disable a trigger?

You can use the **ALTER TRIGGER** statement with the **ENABLE** or **DISABLE** option to enable or disable a trigger.

Question 6

What are some potential drawbacks of using triggers?

Triggers can introduce hidden logic that may be harder to track and debug. Overuse of triggers can lead to performance issues and make the codebase harder to maintain.

Question 7

How do you create a view in SQL?

To create a view in SQL, you use the **CREATE VIEW** statement, providing a name for the view and the SELECT query that defines the view's data.

Question 8

Can you update data through a view? If yes, what are the restrictions?

Yes, you can update data through a view under certain conditions. The view must be updatable, meaning it must meet specific criteria, such as having a single table in the FROM clause, not containing aggregate functions, and not having certain constructs like GROUP BY or HAVING.

Question 9

What is the difference between a regular view and a materialized view?

A regular view is a virtual table that displays the results of a SELECT query. A materialized view, on the other hand, physically stores the results of a query, providing faster data retrieval at the cost of potentially stale data.

Question 10
How can you update a materialized view?

Materialized views are updated automatically based on their refresh settings (e.g., on demand, at specified intervals, or when underlying data changes).

Question 11
What is a nested view, and how does it differ from a regular view?

A nested view is a view that is based on another view. It creates a layered abstraction over the data, allowing for more complex queries.

Question 12
In what situations would you use an indexed view?

Indexed views are beneficial when you have complex queries that involve aggregations or joins on large datasets, as they can significantly improve query performance.

Question 13
How do views contribute to data security and access control?

Views allow you to grant users access to specific columns or rows, hiding sensitive data and enforcing security at the database level.

Question 14
Can you combine views with joins in a query?

Yes, you can use views in combination with joins to simplify complex queries and avoid redundancy in the code.

Question 15

How does recursion work in views, and what is its use case?

Recursive views enable hierarchical querying, where a view refers to itself to traverse hierarchical data structures, such as organizational charts or bill of materials.

Question 16

What is the impact of updating the underlying tables on views?

Updating the underlying tables may change the data presented by views. However, if the views are read-only or restrict certain modifications, changes to the underlying tables will not be allowed.

Question 17

How can you handle updates on non-updatable views?

You can use INSTEAD OF triggers to handle updates on non-updatable views, specifying the logic to perform the update on the underlying tables.

Question 18

How do views contribute to data abstraction and query simplification?

Views provide a level of data abstraction by allowing users to interact with the data using a simplified virtual table, without exposing the complexity of underlying tables.

Question 19

Can you provide an example of a situation where a trigger would be useful?

One example is maintaining an audit trail. A trigger could automatically insert a record into an audit table whenever a specific table is updated.

Question 20

How would you create an indexed view to improve query performance?

To create an indexed view, you would define the view and then use the **CREATE INDEX** statement to create an index on the view's columns, optimizing query execution.

These questions cover a wide range of topics related to database triggers and views. Preparing for these questions will help you gain a comprehensive understanding of triggers and views and their practical application in database design and query optimization.

CHAPTER 10

Normalization

Database normalization is a fundamental concept in database design that aims to organize data efficiently and eliminate redundancy. It helps maintain data integrity by reducing data anomalies and ensuring that data is stored in a structured, logical manner. By following the principles of normalization, you can design databases that are easy to maintain, update, and expand while avoiding data inconsistencies.

In this chapter, we will explore the world of database normalization and delve into the essential topics that form the foundation of data integrity. Whether you are a database administrator, a data analyst, or a database developer, understanding normalization principles is crucial for creating robust and reliable databases.

Important Topics to Prepare on Database Normalization:

1. **Introduction to Normalization**: Understanding the concept of database normalization, its purpose, and the advantages it brings to database design.

2. **First Normal Form (1NF)**: Grasping the principles of 1NF, which involves eliminating duplicate columns and ensuring atomicity of data.

3. **Second Normal Form (2NF)**: Learning how to achieve 2NF by removing partial dependencies and creating separate tables for related data.

4. **Third Normal Form (3NF)**: Understanding the process of reaching 3NF by eliminating transitive dependencies, ensuring data is only stored in one place.

5. **Boyce-Codd Normal Form (BCNF)**: Exploring BCNF, a higher level of normalization that addresses anomalies related to functional dependencies.

6. **Fourth Normal Form (4NF)**: Discovering 4NF, which deals with multi-valued dependencies and ensures that each field depends only on the entire primary key.

7. **Fifth Normal Form (5NF)**: Understanding 5NF, also known as Project-Join Normal Form (PJ/NF), which addresses join dependencies between candidate keys.

8. **Denormalization**: Learning about denormalization, when it is appropriate to use, and its impact on performance and data integrity.

9. **Anomalies in Data**: Identifying various data anomalies like insertion, update, and deletion anomalies, and how normalization helps mitigate them.

10. **Composite Keys and Surrogate Keys**: Understanding the use of composite keys and surrogate keys as primary keys in normalization.

11. **Functional Dependencies**: Grasping the concept of functional dependencies, which forms the basis for normalization rules.

12. **Normalization vs. Performance**: Analyzing the trade-off between normalization and query performance, and how to strike a balance in database design.

13. **Normalization in Real-World Scenarios**: Exploring real-world examples where normalization is applied to ensure data integrity, such as e-commerce websites, inventory management systems, and customer relationship management (CRM) databases.

14. **Normalization Guidelines**: Learning practical guidelines and best practices for applying normalization principles effectively in database design.

15. **Normalization and Data Modeling**: Understanding the relationship between normalization and data modeling, and how normalization enhances data modeling outcomes.

16. **Normalization and Indexing**: Analyzing the impact of normalization on indexing strategies and database query performance.

17. **Normalization and Data Redundancy**: Understanding how normalization eliminates data redundancy, leading to optimized storage and maintenance.

18. **Database Normalization Tools**: Familiarizing yourself with tools and utilities that aid in assessing and validating the normalization process.

Database normalization is a crucial aspect of designing efficient and robust databases. By mastering the principles and topics mentioned above, you can create databases that are resilient, scalable, and maintainable. Normalization ensures that data remains consistent and accurate throughout its lifecycle, making it an indispensable skill for any database professional.

In the subsequent sections, we will delve into each of these topics, providing you with in-depth knowledge and practical insights into database normalization and data integrity. Let's embark on this journey into the realm of database normalization and its significance in building reliable and efficient databases!

Below are 20+ questions on database normalization and data integrity, along with their answers:

Question 1

What is database normalization, and why is it essential in database design?

Database normalization is the process of organizing data in a database to reduce redundancy and data anomalies. It ensures data integrity, minimizes data duplication, and makes the database more efficient and maintainable.

Question 2

Explain the First Normal Form (1NF) and its requirements.

1NF requires that each table cell contains a single value (atomicity) and that there are no repeating groups or duplicate rows in the table.

Question 3

How does the Second Normal Form (2NF) differ from 1NF, and what problem does it address?

2NF addresses the issue of partial dependencies by requiring that non-key attributes be fully dependent on the entire primary key.

Question 4

What is the Third Normal Form (3NF), and what types of dependencies does it eliminate?

3NF eliminates transitive dependencies, ensuring that non-key attributes are dependent only on the primary key and not on other non-key attributes.

Question 5

When should you consider moving to Boyce-Codd Normal Form (BCNF) instead of 3NF?

BCNF should be considered when a table has overlapping candidate keys and is in 3NF but still contains anomalies due to functional dependencies.

Question 6

What is Fourth Normal Form (4NF), and what problem does it address?

4NF addresses multi-valued dependencies and ensures that each non-key attribute is dependent only on the entire primary key, not on subsets of the primary key.

Question 7

How does Fifth Normal Form (5NF) handle join dependencies?

5NF addresses join dependencies, ensuring that there are no redundant combinations of attributes in separate tables.

Question 8

What is denormalization, and in what situations is it appropriate to use?

Denormalization involves deliberately introducing redundancy into a database to improve query performance. It is suitable for read-heavy applications or situations where query optimization is crucial.

Question 9

How does normalization help in avoiding insertion, update, and deletion anomalies?

Normalization reduces or eliminates data anomalies by ensuring that data is stored logically and without redundancy, preventing data inconsistencies during insert, update, and delete operations.

Question 10

What is the purpose of functional dependencies in normalization?

Functional dependencies define the relationships between attributes in a table and form the basis for normalization rules.

Question 11

Can you have multiple candidate keys in a table, and how do they relate to normalization?

Yes, a table can have multiple candidate keys. They are used to determine if the table is in the desired normal form and are essential for normalization.

Question 12

How does normalization impact database query performance?

Normalization can improve data integrity but may lead to more complex joins and potentially slower query performance. Denormalization is sometimes used to enhance query performance.

Question 13

What are the potential drawbacks of denormalization?

Denormalization can lead to data redundancy, making updates and maintenance more challenging. It can also increase the risk of data inconsistencies if not managed properly.

Question 14

In what real-world scenarios is normalization crucial for data integrity?

Normalization is crucial in scenarios such as e-commerce websites (managing product catalogs), inventory management systems, and customer relationship management (CRM) databases (tracking customer interactions).

Question 15

How can you decide on the level of normalization required for a specific database design?

The level of normalization required depends on the specific requirements of the application. Striking a balance between normalization and denormalization is crucial to meet performance and data integrity needs.

Question 16

Can you provide an example of a table that violates the First Normal Form (1NF)?

A table with repeating groups or multiple values in a single cell violates 1NF.

For example:

```
Student (student_id, name, subject1, subject2,
subject3)
```

Question 17

How would you convert the above table into 1NF?

To convert the table into 1NF, we would split the subjects into separate rows, each with its own student_id and name:

```
Student (student_id, name) Subject (student_id,
subject)
```

Question 18

Explain the process of achieving Second Normal Form (2NF) in a table.

To achieve 2NF, you need to identify and remove partial dependencies by breaking down the table into separate tables for each subset of dependent attributes.

Question 19

What is a composite key, and when is it used in normalization?

A composite key is a primary key that consists of more than one attribute. It is used when no single attribute can uniquely identify a row, but a combination of attributes can.

Question 20

How can normalization and denormalization be balanced in a database design?

Balancing normalization and denormalization involves understanding the specific requirements of the application and deciding which tables need to be normalized for data integrity and which can be denormalized for performance optimization.

These questions cover various aspects of database normalization and data integrity. By preparing for these questions, you can gain a comprehensive understanding of normalization principles and their practical application in database design.

Chapter 11

Transaction

In the realm of database management systems, transactions play a crucial role in ensuring data integrity, consistency, and reliability. A transaction is a logical unit of work that comprises one or more database operations, executed as a single, indivisible unit. By providing a "all-or-nothing" approach, transactions either fully commit changes to the database or entirely roll back all changes in case of failure or error.

In this chapter, we will delve into the intricacies of database transactions and explore how they maintain data integrity while supporting concurrent access to the database. Understanding transaction concepts and management is vital for database administrators, developers, and anyone dealing with critical data operations.

Important Topics to Prepare on Database Transactions:

1. **Transaction Basics**: Understanding the fundamental concepts of transactions, their properties (ACID), and their significance in the database world.

2. **ACID Properties**: Grasping the four essential properties of transactions: Atomicity, Consistency, Isolation, and Durability.

3. **Transaction States**: Learning about the various states that a transaction can undergo during its lifecycle: Active, Partially Committed, Committed, Failed, and Aborted.

4. **Transaction Management**: Exploring how databases manage transactions, log changes, and ensure data integrity.

5. **BEGIN, COMMIT, and ROLLBACK**: Understanding the SQL commands used to initiate, commit, and roll back transactions.

6. **Implicit vs. Explicit Transactions**: Differentiating between implicit transactions (auto-commit) and explicit transactions (manually initiated and controlled).

7. **Nested Transactions**: Understanding the concept of nested transactions and their behavior within a transactional environment.

8. **Savepoints**: Exploring the use of savepoints within transactions to provide finer control over rollback operations.

9. **Isolation Levels**: Understanding the different isolation levels (Read Uncommitted, Read Committed, Repeatable Read, Serializable) and their impact on data consistency and concurrency.

10. **Dirty Read, Non-Repeatable Read, and Phantom Read**: Understanding various phenomena that can occur due to concurrent transactions at different isolation levels.

11. **Deadlocks**: Recognizing deadlocks, their causes, and strategies to avoid and resolve them.

12. **Transaction Locking**: Exploring the concept of locking to manage concurrent access to resources and maintain data consistency.

13. **Transaction Logging**: Understanding transaction log files and their role in database recovery and rollback operations.

14. **Error Handling in Transactions**: Learning how to handle errors within transactions to ensure proper rollback and recovery.

15. **Two-Phase Commit (2PC)**: Understanding the 2PC protocol for coordinating distributed transactions.

16. **Transaction Management in Stored Procedures**: Exploring how transactions are handled within stored procedures and functions.

17. **Concurrency Control**: Understanding the techniques used to manage concurrent access to data, including optimistic and pessimistic concurrency control.

18. **Data Integrity and Constraints**: Recognizing how transactions help enforce data integrity through constraints and validation.

19. **Transaction Best Practices**: Learning best practices for designing and managing transactions effectively in different scenarios.

20. **Real-World Use Cases**: Exploring real-world examples where transactions are crucial for data consistency and reliability, such as online banking, e-commerce, and inventory management.

Database transactions are the cornerstone of data integrity and consistency in modern database systems. By mastering the concepts and practices of transactions, you can ensure the reliability and accuracy of your database operations, making you a proficient and confident database professional.

In the following chapters, we will explore each of these topics in detail, providing you with a comprehensive understanding of database transactions and their vital role in the database management process. Let's delve into the world of database transactions and transaction management!

Below are some common SQL transaction-related questions that are often asked in interviews:

Question 1

What is a transaction in the context of a database?

A transaction in a database is a logical unit of work that consists of one or more database operations. It is executed as a single, indivisible unit, ensuring data integrity and consistency.

Question 2

Explain the ACID properties of transactions.

ACID stands for Atomicity, Consistency, Isolation, and Durability:

- Atomicity ensures that a transaction is treated as a single unit of work, either fully committed or fully rolled back in case of failure.
- Consistency ensures that the database remains in a valid state before and after the transaction.
- Isolation ensures that each transaction is executed independently of other transactions, preventing interference and preserving data integrity.
- Durability ensures that the changes made by a committed transaction are permanent and survive system failures.

Question 3

What are the different states that a transaction can go through during its lifecycle?

A transaction can go through the following states: Active, Partially Committed, Committed, Failed, and Aborted.

Question 4

How do you begin a transaction in SQL, and how do you end it?

In SQL, you can begin a transaction using the BEGIN TRANSACTION or START TRANSACTION statement. To end a transaction, you can use the COMMIT statement to save the changes or the ROLLBACK statement to discard the changes.

Question 5

What is the difference between an implicit transaction and an explicit transaction?

An implicit transaction (auto-commit) is automatically started and committed for each individual SQL statement, while an explicit transaction (manually controlled) requires the use of **BEGIN TRANSACTION**, **COMMIT**, and **ROLLBACK** statements.

Question 6

Explain the concept of savepoints in transactions.

Savepoints allow you to create named markers within a transaction, enabling you to roll back to a specific point within the transaction if needed.

Question 7

What is a deadlock in transactions, and how can it be resolved?

A deadlock occurs when two or more transactions are blocked, each waiting for a resource held by the other. Deadlocks can be resolved by setting transaction priorities, using timeouts, or by automatically rolling back one of the conflicting transactions.

Question 8

What are the different isolation levels in transactions, and how do they affect data consistency and concurrency?

The isolation levels are Read Uncommitted, Read Committed, Repeatable Read, and Serializable. Each level provides different levels of data consistency and concurrency control, with higher levels offering stronger isolation but potentially impacting performance.

Question 9

How can you handle errors within transactions to ensure proper rollback and recovery?

Error handling within transactions involves using **TRY...CATCH** blocks (in SQL Server) or **EXCEPTION** blocks (in PostgreSQL) to catch and handle errors gracefully. If an error occurs, the transaction can be rolled back to avoid leaving the database in an inconsistent state.

Question 10

What is the purpose of a transaction log in a database, and how does it aid in recovery?

The transaction log records all changes made to the database during a transaction. It helps in database recovery by allowing the system to roll back uncommitted changes or roll forward committed changes in case of a system failure or crash.

Question 11

How can you implement a two-phase commit (2PC) protocol for coordinating distributed transactions?

The two-phase commit protocol involves a coordinator and multiple participants (distributed systems). In the first phase, the coordinator asks all participants if they can commit the transaction. In the second phase, the coordinator instructs all participants to either commit or abort the transaction based on the responses received.

Question 12

What are the best practices for designing and managing transactions effectively?

Some best practices include keeping transactions short and focused, using appropriate isolation levels, avoiding long-running transactions, and ensuring proper error handling and rollback procedures.

These questions cover a wide range of topics related to SQL transactions and transaction management. Preparing for these questions will help you gain a thorough understanding of how transactions work, their importance in maintaining data integrity, and how to handle various transaction-related scenarios.

CHAPTER 12

Window Function and CTE

In the world of database querying and analysis, SQL Window Functions and Common Table Expressions (CTEs) are powerful tools that provide advanced analytical capabilities and aid in writing complex yet efficient queries.

Window Functions enable you to perform calculations across rows within a defined window or partition of the result set, allowing for insightful data insights and comparisons. On the other hand, CTEs provide a way to create temporary result sets for more readable and modular queries, making SQL code easier to maintain.

In this chapter, we will explore SQL Window Functions and CTEs, unraveling their potential and usefulness in solving a variety of data manipulation tasks.

Whether you are an aspiring data analyst or an experienced database professional, understanding these concepts will elevate your SQL skills to new heights, empowering you to tackle challenging analytical queries and optimize your data querying experience.

Important Topics to Prepare on Window Functions and CTEs:

1. **Window Functions Overview**: Understanding the concept of Window Functions, their syntax, and how they differ from regular aggregate functions.

2. **PARTITION BY Clause**: Learning how to use the **PARTITION BY** clause to divide the result set into partitions or groups for Window Functions calculations.

3. **ORDER BY Clause**: Exploring the **ORDER BY** clause within Window Functions to specify the sorting order for the window frame.

4. **ROWS/RANGE Clause**: Differentiating between the **ROWS** and **RANGE** clauses in Window Functions and their impact on the window frame definition.

5. **Common Window Functions**: Familiarizing yourself with common Window Functions like **ROW_NUMBER, RANK, DENSE_RANK, LEAD, LAG, SUM, AVG, MAX, MIN**, and others.

6. **Aggregation with Window Functions**: Understanding how to combine Window Functions with aggregate functions to perform advanced analytical calculations.

7. **Window Frames**: Learning about various window frame options, such as **ROWS BETWEEN, RANGE BETWEEN,** and **UNBOUNDED PRECEDING/UNBOUNDED FOLLOWING,** to customize the window scope.

8. **CTE Overview**: Grasping the concept of Common Table Expressions (CTEs), their syntax, and how they simplify complex queries.

9. **Recursive CTEs**: Exploring the concept of Recursive CTEs, which allow you to perform recursive queries and solve hierarchical problems.

10. **Multiple CTEs**: Understanding how to use multiple CTEs in a single query to break down complex logic into manageable components.

11. **Nested CTEs**: Learning how to nest CTEs inside each other to build modular and reusable query components.

12. **CTEs vs. Subqueries**: Comparing CTEs with subqueries and understanding when to use each approach.

13. **Performance Considerations**: Analyzing the performance implications of using Window Functions and CTEs in SQL queries and identifying potential optimizations.

14. **Real-World Use Cases**: Exploring real-world scenarios where Window Functions and CTEs shine, such as ranking results, handling time series data, and solving recursive problems.

15. **Combining Window Functions and CTEs**: Discovering the synergy between Window Functions and CTEs in complex analytical queries.

SQL Window Functions and CTEs are indispensable tools for data analysts, database administrators, and anyone involved in querying and analysing data. With these advanced SQL features in your toolkit, you can elevate your data analysis capabilities, gain deeper insights from your data, and craft sophisticated queries with ease.

Let's embark on this journey into the world of SQL Window Functions and CTEs, unlocking the full potential of your SQL querying skills!

Below are 20+ SQL questions covering the topics of Window Functions and Common Table Expressions (CTEs), along with their answers:

Question 1

What are Window Functions in SQL, and how are they different from regular aggregate functions?

Window Functions perform calculations across rows within a defined window or partition of the result set, without collapsing the result into a single row. Unlike regular aggregate functions, Window Functions preserve individual rows and return results alongside the original data.

Question 2

Explain the PARTITION BY clause in Window Functions with an example.

The **PARTITION BY** clause divides the result set into partitions or groups, and the Window Function operates on each partition independently.

For example:

```
SELECT
    employee_id,
    department,
    salary,
    RANK() OVER (PARTITION BY department ORDER BY salary DESC) AS salary_ran
FROM
    employees;
```

In this query, we use the **RANK()** function with the **OVER** clause to assign a rank to each employee within their respective department based on their salary in descending order. The **PARTITION BY department** clause divides the result set into partitions based on the **department** column, and then the **ORDER BY salary DESC** specifies the order in which salaries are ranked within each department. The result will display the **employee_id**, **department**, **salary**, and **salary_rank** for each employee.

Question 3

How do you calculate the cumulative salary for each department using Window Functions?

You can use the **SUM()** function with the **PARTITION BY** clause to calculate the cumulative salary within each department. For example:

```
SELECT
    employee_id,
    department,
    salary,
    SUM(salary) OVER (PARTITION BY department ORDER BY employee_id) AS cumul
FROM
    employees;
```

In this query, the **SUM()** function is used with the **OVER** clause to calculate the cumulative salary for each employee within their respective department. The **PARTITION BY department** clause divides the result set into partitions based on the **department** column, and the **ORDER BY employee_id** specifies the order in which the cumulative sum is calculated. The result will display the **employee_id**, **department**, **salary**, and **cumulative_salary** for each employee, showing the running total of salaries within each department.

Question 4

What is the purpose of the ORDER BY clause in Window Functions?

The **ORDER BY** clause within Window Functions defines the sorting order of rows in the window frame. It is crucial to ensure consistent and meaningful results for Window Functions.

Question 5

How can you find the percentage of total sales for each product using Window Functions?

You can use the **SUM()** function with the **OVER()** clause to calculate the total sales and then divide individual sales by the total to get the percentage.

```
SELECT
    product_id,
    sales,
    sales / SUM(sales) OVER () * 100 AS percentage_of_total_sales
FROM
    sales_table;
```

In this query, the **SUM()** function with the **OVER** clause is used to calculate the total sum of sales across the entire **sales_table**. Then, the **percentage_of_total_sales** is calculated for each product by dividing its individual **sales** by the total sum of sales and multiplying by 100. The result will display the **product_id**, **sales**, and **percentage_of_total_sales** for each product, showing its contribution as a percentage of the total sales.

Question 6

What is the difference between ROWS BETWEEN and RANGE BETWEEN clauses in Window Functions?

The **ROWS BETWEEN** clause defines the frame based on the number of rows, whereas the **RANGE BETWEEN** clauses defines the frame based on the actual values within the window.

Question 7

How do you find the lead and lag values for a column using Window Functions?

You can use the **LEAD()** and **LAG()** functions to access the subsequent and previous values, respectively, for a given column.

```
SELECT
    employee_id,
    name,
    salary,
    LEAD(salary) OVER (ORDER BY salary) AS next_salary,
    LAG(salary) OVER (ORDER BY salary) AS previous_salary
FROM
    employees;
```

In this query, the **LEAD()** and **LAG()** functions with the **OVER** clause are used to retrieve the next and previous salary values for each employee, respectively. The **ORDER BY salary** clause specifies the order in which the values are retrieved. The result will display the **employee_id**, **name**, **salary**, **next_salary**, and **previous_salary** for each employee, showing the adjacent salaries in ascending order.

Question 8

Explain the concept of Recursive CTEs in SQL.

Recursive CTEs allow you to perform recursive queries, where a query refers to its own result set in a subsequent iteration. It is commonly used for hierarchical data, such as organizational structures or nested categories.

Question 9

How do you use a Recursive CTE to traverse a hierarchical table?

You need to define two parts in the CTE: the anchor member that selects the starting point of recursion, and the recursive member that joins the result of the previous iteration.

```
WITH RECURSIVE cte_hierarchy AS
(
    -- Anchor member
    SELECT employee_id, name, manager_id, 0 AS level
    FROM employees
    WHERE manager_id IS NULL

    UNION ALL

    -- Recursive member
    SELECT e.employee_id, e.name, e.manager_id, cte.level + 1
    FROM employees e
    JOIN cte_hierarchy cte ON e.manager_id = cte.employee_id
)

SELECT *
FROM cte_hierarchy;
```

The query uses a CTE named **cte_hierarchy** to perform a recursive traversal of the employee hierarchy stored in the **employees** table. The anchor member selects the top-level employees (those with **manager_id** set to NULL), and the recursive member joins the CTE with the **employees** table to retrieve the subordinates of each employee, incrementing the **level** in the process.

The final result is a hierarchical representation of the employees and their relationships in the table. The output will include columns for **employee_id**, **name**, **manager_id**, and the **level** in the hierarchy for each employee.

For example, the output might look like this:

```
employee_id | name      | manager_id | level
----------------------------------------------------
1           | John      | NULL       | 0
2           | Mary      | 1          | 1
3           | Alice     | 2          | 2
4           | Bob       | 2          | 2
5           | Sarah     | 1          | 1
6           | David     | 5          | 2
7           | Linda     | 6          | 3
8           | Michael   | NULL       | 0
9           | James     | 8          | 1
```

Question 10

How can you use a CTE to simplify a complex query?

CTEs can modularize complex queries by breaking them down into more manageable components. They make the code more readable, maintainable, and reusable.

Question 11

When would you use a CTE instead of a subquery?

CTEs are preferable over subqueries when you need to use the same subquery multiple times within a larger query, as CTEs eliminate the need to repeat the subquery.

Question 12

How can you use multiple CTEs in a single query?

You can define multiple CTEs separated by commas before the main query. Each CTE should have a unique name. For example:

```
WITH cte1 AS (...), cte2 AS (...) SELECT ... FROM ...
```

Question 13

Can you use a CTE inside another CTE?

Yes, you can nest CTEs inside each other to build more modular and reusable query components.

Question 14

How do you perform aggregation on CTEs?

You can perform aggregation on the result of a CTE just like any other table.

<u>For example:</u>

```
WITH cte_sales AS
(
    SELECT product_id, SUM(sales) AS total_sales
    FROM sales_table
    GROUP BY product_id
)

SELECT *
FROM cte_sales;
```

The query uses a Common Table Expression (CTE) named **cte_sales** to calculate the total sales for each product from the **sales_table**. The CTE computes the sum of sales for each product by grouping the data based on the **product_id**.

The final result will display the **product_id** and the corresponding **total_sales** for each product, providing a summary of the sales data by product.

Question 15

How do you calculate the running total for a column using Window Functions and CTEs?

You can use the **SUM()** function with the **OVER()** clause inside a CTE to calculate the running total. For example:

```
WITH cte_running_total AS
(
    SELECT order_id, order_date, order_amount,
           SUM(order_amount) OVER (ORDER BY order_date) AS running_total
    FROM orders
)

SELECT *
FROM cte_running_total;
```

The query uses a Common Table Expression (CTE) named cte_running_total to calculate the running total of order_amount for each order from the orders table. The SUM function with the OVER clause and ORDER BY is used to calculate the cumulative sum of order_amount up to the current row, based on the order_date order.

The final result will display columns for order_id, order_date, order_amount, and the **running_total**, which represents the cumulative sum of **order_amount** up to each order's **order_date**. This provides an overview of the running total of sales over time.

Question 16

How can you use a Window Function with a PARTITION BY clause to find the highest salary in each department?

You can use the **PARTITION BY** clause along with the **MAX()** function to find the highest salary within each department.

For example:

```
SELECT
    employee_id,
    department,
    salary,
    MAX(salary) OVER (PARTITION BY department) AS highest_salary
FROM employees;
```

In this query, we use the **MAX()** function with the **OVER** clause to calculate the highest salary within each department using the

PARTITION BY clause. The OVER (PARTITION BY department) part divides the result set into partitions based on the department column, and then the MAX(salary) function is applied within each partition to get the highest salary for that specific department. The result will show each employee's employee_id, department, salary, and the highest salary within their respective department as highest_salary.

Question 17

How do you calculate the percentage change in sales compared to the previous month using Window Functions?

You can use the LAG() function to access the previous month's sales and then calculate the percentage change.

For example:

```
SELECT
    month,
    sales,
    (sales - LAG(sales) OVER (ORDER BY month)) / LAG(sales) OVER (ORDER BY
FROM
    monthly_sales;
```

In this query, we use the LAG() function with the OVER clause to calculate the percentage change in sales from one month to the next. The LAG(sales) OVER (ORDER BY month) part fetches the sales value of the previous row based on the month order, and then the percentage change is calculated as (sales - previous_sales) / previous_sales * 100.

The result will show each month, the corresponding sales, and the percentage_change, which represents the percentage change in sales compared to the previous month.

Question 18

How can you use the RANK() function to find the top N employees with the highest salary?

You can use the **RANK()** function along with a Common Table Expression (CTE) to find the top N employees with the highest salary. Here's how you can do it:

```sql
WITH RankedEmployees AS (
    SELECT
        employee_id,
        name,
        salary,
        RANK() OVER (ORDER BY salary DESC) AS salary_rank
    FROM
        employees
)
SELECT
    employee_id,
    name,
    salary
FROM
    RankedEmployees
WHERE
    salary_rank <= N;
```

Replace **N** with the desired number to retrieve the top N employees.

In this query:

1. The **RankedEmployees** CTE assigns a rank to each employee based on their salary in descending order using the **RANK()** function with the **OVER** clause.
2. The outer **SELECT** statement retrieves the **employee_id**, **name**, and **salary** columns from the **RankedEmployees** CTE for employees whose **salary_rank** is less than or equal to **N**. This will give you the top N employees with the highest salary.

The result will display the details of the top N employees with the highest salary, based on the specified value of **N**.

Question 19

Explain the concept of a "rolling sum" using Window Functions.

A "rolling sum" calculates the sum of a column for a specific range of rows, usually with an **ORDER BY** clause to define the order of rows. It is useful for time series analysis or calculating moving averages.

Question 20

How do you use the ROWS BETWEEN clause to calculate a "rolling sum"?

You can use the **ROWS BETWEEN** clause with **ORDER BY** to define the range of rows for the "rolling sum." For example, to calculate a sum of the last three rows:

```
SELECT
    date,
    sales,
    SUM(sales) OVER (ORDER BY date ROWS BETWEEN 2 PRECEDING AND CURRENT ROW)
        AS rolling_sum
FROM
    sales_data;
```

In this query, the **SUM()** function with the **OVER** clause is used to calculate the rolling sum of sales over a window of three rows: the current row and the two preceding rows, ordered by the **date** column. The result will display the **date**, **sales**, and **rolling_sum** for each row in the **sales_data** table, showing the cumulative sum of sales over the specified window.

Question 21

What are the performance considerations when using Window Functions and CTEs in SQL?

Using Window Functions and CTEs can impact query performance, especially when dealing with large datasets. It's essential to consider appropriate indexing and analyze query execution plans to optimize performance.

Question 22

How can you use Window Functions and CTEs together in a single query to perform advanced analytical calculations?

You can use CTEs to prepare the data and then apply Window Functions on the CTE result set to perform complex calculations. For example:

```
WITH cte_sales AS
(
    SELECT product_id, SUM(sales) AS total_sales
    FROM sales_table
    GROUP BY product_id
)
SELECT
    product_id,
    total_sales,
    total_sales / SUM(total_sales) OVER () * 100 AS percentage_of_total_sale
FROM
    cte_sales;
```

In this query, a Common Table Expression (CTE) named **cte_sales** is used to calculate the total sales for each product from the **sales_table**.

The **SUM()** function with the **OVER** clause is used to calculate the total sum of sales across the entire **cte_sales** result set.

Then, the **percentage_of_total_sales** is calculated for each product by dividing its individual **total_sales** by the total sum of sales and multiplying by 100. The result will display the **product_id**, **total_sales**, and **percentage_of_total_sales** for each product, showing its contribution as a percentage of the total sales.

Question 23

How do you use Window Functions to find the top N products with the highest sales, considering ties?

You can use the **DENSE_RANK()** function to handle ties and rank the products accordingly. For example:

```
SELECT
    product_id,
    sales
FROM
    (
        SELECT
            product_id,
            sales,
            DENSE_RANK() OVER (ORDER BY sales DESC) AS sales_rank
        FROM
            sales_table
    ) ranked_sales
WHERE
    sales_rank <= N;
```

In this query:

1. The inner subquery calculates the **sales_rank** for each product based on their sales in descending order using the **DENSE_RANK()** function with the **OVER** clause. The result of this subquery is aliased as **ranked_sales**.

2. The outer **SELECT** statement retrieves the **product_id** and **sales** columns from the **ranked_sales** subquery for products whose **sales_rank** is less than or equal to **N**. This will give you the top N products with the highest sales.

Replace **N** with the desired number of top products you want to retrieve.

Question 24

How can you calculate the average salary for each department while excluding the highest and lowest salaries using Window Functions?

You can use the **RANK()** function with **PARTITION BY** to rank salaries within each department and then filter out the highest and lowest ranks in a subquery. For example:

```
SELECT
    department,
    AVG(salary) AS average_salary
FROM
    (
        SELECT
            department,
            salary,
            RANK() OVER (PARTITION BY department ORDER BY salary) AS salary_
        FROM
            employees
    ) ranked_employees
WHERE
    salary_rank > 1
    AND salary_rank < (SELECT COUNT(DISTINCT salary) FROM employees);
```

In this query:

1. The inner subquery calculates the **salary_rank** for each employee within their respective department based on their salary using the **RANK()** function with the **OVER** clause. The result of this subquery is aliased as **ranked_employees**.

2. The outer **SELECT** statement retrieves the **department** and the average salary (**average_salary**) for departments where the **salary_rank** is greater than 1 and less than the total number of distinct salary values in the **employees** table. This filters out the employees with the highest and lowest salaries within each department.

The result will display the **department** and the average salary for departments where employees' salaries are not the highest or the lowest within their respective departments.

Question 25

How do you find the top N products with the highest sales for each month using Window Functions?

You can use the **PARTITION BY** clause with the **RANK()** function to rank products within each month and then filter the results using a subquery.

<u>For example:</u>

```sql
SELECT
    month,
    product_id,
    sales
FROM
    (
        SELECT
            month,
            product_id,
            sales,
            RANK() OVER (PARTITION BY month ORDER BY sales DESC) AS sales_rank
        FROM
            monthly_sales
    ) ranked_sales
WHERE
    sales_rank <= N;
```

```sql
SELECT
    month,
    product_id,
    sales
FROM
    (
        SELECT
            month,
            product_id,
            sales,
            RANK() OVER (PARTITION BY month ORDER BY sales DESC) AS sales_rank
        FROM
            monthly_sales
    ) ranked_sales
WHERE
    sales_rank <= N;
```

In this query:

1. The inner subquery calculates the **sales_rank** for each product within each month based on their sales in descending order using the **RANK()** function with the **OVER** clause. The result of this subquery is aliased as **ranked_sales**.

2. The outer **SELECT** statement retrieves the **month**, **product_id**, and **sales** columns from the **ranked_sales** subquery for products whose **sales_rank** is less than or equal to **N**. This will give you the top N products with the highest sales for each month.

189

Replace **N** with the desired number of top products you want to retrieve for each month.

Question 26

What are the potential use cases for Recursive CTEs, and how do they work?

Recursive CTEs are useful for working with hierarchical data, such as organizational charts, bill of materials, or nested categories. They consist of two parts: the anchor member and the recursive member, and they repeatedly execute the recursive member until it returns no rows.

Question 27

How can you use a Recursive CTE to traverse a hierarchical table with unlimited nesting levels?

You can use the **UNION ALL** operator in the recursive member to repeatedly join the CTE with itself.

For example:

```sql
WITH RECURSIVE cte_hierarchy AS (
    -- Anchor member
    SELECT category_id, category_name, parent_category_id, 1 AS level
    FROM categories
    WHERE parent_category_id IS NULL

    UNION ALL

    -- Recursive member
    SELECT c.category_id, c.category_name, c.parent_category_id, h.level + 1
    FROM categories c
    JOIN cte_hierarchy h ON c.parent_category_id = h.category_id
)
SELECT *
FROM cte_hierarchy;
```

In this query:

1. The **WITH RECURSIVE** clause starts a common table expression (CTE) named **cte_hierarchy** that will hold the hierarchical data.

2. The first part is the "Anchor member" of the recursive query, which selects the root categories where **parent_category_id** is **NULL** and assigns them a level of **1**.

3. The **UNION ALL** combines the anchor member with the "Recursive member," which selects child categories and joins them with the previous level's results to build the hierarchy. The level is incremented by 1.

4. The **SELECT * FROM cte_hierarchy** retrieves all columns from the **cte_hierarchy** CTE, displaying the hierarchical data.

This query uses a recursive CTE to traverse a category hierarchy, starting from root categories and progressing to their child categories. The result will show the entire hierarchy with columns **category_id**, **category_name**, **parent_category_id**, and **level** indicating the hierarchy level.

Question 28

How can you use the SUM() function with PARTITION BY and ORDER BY to calculate the moving average of sales for each product?

You can use the **SUM()** function with **PARTITION BY** to calculate the sum of sales within each product and then use the **ORDER BY** clause to specify the order of sales.

For example:

```
SELECT
    product_id,
    sale_date,
    sales,
    AVG(sales) OVER (
        PARTITION BY product_id
        ORDER BY sale_date
        ROWS BETWEEN 2 PRECEDING AND CURRENT ROW
    ) AS moving_average
FROM
    sales_table;
```

In this query:

1. The **SELECT** statement retrieves columns from the **sales_table**: **product_id, sale_date, sales**, and a calculated column named **moving_average**.

2. The **AVG(sales) OVER (...)** calculates the moving average of **sales** for each **product_id** partition. The **PARTITION BY product_id** clause divides the result set into partitions based on the distinct values of **product_id**.

3. The **ORDER BY sale_date** specifies that the moving average is ordered by the **sale_date**.

4. The **ROWS BETWEEN 2 PRECEDING AND CURRENT ROW** clause defines the window frame for the moving average calculation. It includes the current row and the two preceding rows within each partition.

5. The result will display the **product_id, sale_date, sales**, and **moving_average** columns for each row in the **sales_table**, showing the average of sales for the current row and its two preceding rows within each product partition.

Question 29

How do you use a CTE to simplify a query that involves multiple subqueries?

You can create CTEs for each subquery and then reference them in the main query, making the code more concise and easier to understand.

Question 30

How can you use the ROWS UNBOUNDED PRECEDING and ROWS UNBOUNDED FOLLOWING clauses in Window Functions?

The **ROWS UNBOUNDED PRECEDING** and **ROWS UNBOUNDED FOLLOWING** clauses in Window Functions allow you to specify an unbounded window frame that includes all rows from the beginning (preceding) or end (following) of the partition, respectively.

For example, let's say you want to calculate the running total of sales for each product, considering all previous sales.

You can use the **SUM()** function with the **ORDER BY** clause and the unbounded window frame to achieve this:

```sql
SELECT
    product_id,
    sale_date,
    sales,
    SUM(sales) OVER (
        PARTITION BY product_id
        ORDER BY sale_date
        ROWS BETWEEN UNBOUNDED PRECEDING AND CURRENT ROW
    ) AS running_total
FROM
    sales_table;
```

In this query, the **ROWS BETWEEN UNBOUNDED PRECEDING AND CURRENT ROW** clause indicates that the window frame should include all rows from the beginning of the partition up to the current row, allowing the **SUM()** function to calculate the running total for each product.

Question 31

How do you use a CTE to simplify a complex hierarchical query for an organizational chart?

You can create a Recursive CTE to traverse the organizational chart and generate a result set that shows the hierarchical relationships in a more readable and structured format.

Question 32

What is the difference between the DENSE_RANK() and RANK() functions in Window Functions?

The **DENSE_RANK()** function assigns a unique rank to each distinct row, leaving no gaps in the ranking sequence. On the other hand, the **RANK()** function may leave gaps in the ranking sequence when there are ties.

Question 33

How can you use a Window Function to find the percentage of sales contributed by each product compared to the total sales?

You can use the **SUM()** function with the **OVER()** clause to calculate the total sales and then divide the individual sales by the total to get the percentage.

For example:

```sql
SELECT
    product_id,
    sales,
    sales / SUM(sales) OVER () * 100 AS percentage_of_total_sales
FROM
    sales_table;
```

In this query:

1. The SELECT statement retrieves columns from the sales_table: product_id, sales, and a calculated column named percentage_of_total_sales.

2. The SUM(sales) OVER () calculates the total sum of all sales values in the entire result set. The empty parentheses () indicate that there is no specific partitioning for the calculation.

3. The sales / SUM(sales) OVER () * 100 expression calculates the percentage of each sales value compared to the total sum of all sales, and then multiplies by 100 to convert it to a percentage.

4. The result will display the product_id, sales, and percentage_of_total_sales columns for each row in the sales_table, showing how each sale contributes to the total sales percentage.

Question 34

Can you use Window Functions without the PARTITION BY clause? If yes, what will be the result?

Yes, you can use Window Functions without the **PARTITION BY** clause. In this case, the function will treat the entire result set as a single partition, and the calculation will be performed on the entire set of rows.

Question 35

How can you use the RANK() function with the PARTITION BY clause to find the top N employees with the highest salary within each department?

You can use the **RANK()** function with the **PARTITION BY** clause to rank employees based on salary within each department and then filter the results using a subquery.

```
SELECT
    employee_id,
    name,
    department,
    salary
FROM
    (
        SELECT
            employee_id,
            name,
            department,
            salary,
            RANK() OVER (PARTITION BY department ORDER BY salary DESC) AS sa
        FROM
            employees
    ) ranked_employees
WHERE
    salary_rank <= N;
```

In this query:

1. The inner subquery calculates the **salary_rank** for each employee within their respective department based on their salary in descending order using the RANK() function with the OVER clause. The result of this subquery is aliased as ranked_employees.

2. The outer SELECT statement retrieves the employee_id, name, department, and salary columns from the ranked_employees subquery for employees whose salary_rank is less than or equal to N. This will give you the top N employees with the highest salary within each department.

Replace **N** with the desired number to retrieve the top N employees within each department based on their salary ranks.

Question 36

How do you use a Recursive CTE to calculate the total cost of a bill of materials for a product and all its components?

You can create a Recursive CTE that repeatedly joins the product table with the component table until there are no more components, and then calculate the total cost using the **SUM()** function.

Question 37

What are some common performance optimization techniques for queries involving Window Functions and CTEs?

Some common performance optimization techniques include proper indexing, limiting the result set using **WHERE** clauses before applying Window Functions, and avoiding unnecessary ordering when not required.

Question 38

How can you use the FIRST_VALUE() and LAST_VALUE() functions in Window Functions to retrieve the first and last values in a partition?

The **FIRST_VALUE()** function returns the first value in the window frame, while the **LAST_VALUE()** function returns the last value in the window frame.

For example:

```sql
SELECT
    product_id,
    sale_date,
    sales,
    FIRST_VALUE(sales) OVER (
        PARTITION BY product_id
        ORDER BY sale_date
    ) AS first_sale,
    LAST_VALUE(sales) OVER (
        PARTITION BY product_id
        ORDER BY sale_date
    ) AS last_sale
FROM
    sales_table;
```

```
SELECT
    product_id,
    sale_date,
    sales,
    FIRST_VALUE(sales) OVER (
        PARTITION BY product_id
        ORDER BY sale_date
    ) AS first_sale,
    LAST_VALUE(sales) OVER (
        PARTITION BY product_id
        ORDER BY sale_date
    ) AS last_sale
FROM
    sales_table;
```

The query fetches sales data from the **sales_table**. It calculates two things for each row:

1. **first_sale**: The first sale value for each product, ordered by sale date.

2. **last_sale**: The latest sale value for each product, ordered by sale date.

The result shows **product_id**, **sale_date**, **sales**, **first_sale**, and **last_sale** columns. This gives insight into the first and last sales values for each product over time.

Question 39

How do you use Window Functions to calculate the difference between the sales of each product and the average sales of all products?

You can use the **AVG()** function with the **OVER()** clause to calculate the average sales of all products and then subtract the individual sales to find the difference.

For example:

```
SELECT
    product_id,
    sales,
    sales - AVG(sales) OVER () AS sales_difference
FROM
    sales_table;
```

In this query:

1. The **SELECT** statement retrieves columns from the **sales_table**: **product_id**, **sales**, and a calculated column named **sales_difference**.

2. The **AVG(sales) OVER ()** calculates the average of all **sales** values in the entire result set, using the **OVER ()** clause. This means it considers the entire result set as a single partition for the calculation.

3. The **sales - AVG(sales) OVER ()** expression subtracts the overall average sales from each individual **sales** value, resulting in the **sales_difference**.

4. The result will display the **product_id**, **sales**, and **sales_difference** columns for each row in the **sales_table**, showing how much each sale differs from the overall average sales.

Question 40

How can you use Window Functions to calculate the difference in sales between the current and previous months for each product?

You can use the **LAG()** function to access the previous month's sales and then calculate the difference.

For example:

```
SELECT
    product_id,
    sale_date,
    sales,
    sales - LAG(sales) OVER (
        PARTITION BY product_id
        ORDER BY sale_date
    ) AS sales_diff
FROM
    sales_table;
```

In this query:

1. The **LAG()** function with the **OVER** clause is used to calculate the difference between the **sales** of the current row and the previous row within each partition of **product_id**, ordered by **sale_date**.
2. The result will display the **product_id, sale_date, sales**, and **sales_difference** columns for each row in the **sales_table**, showing the difference in sales between the current row and the previous row for each product.

These 40+ SQL questions covering Window Functions and Common Table Expressions (CTEs) will help you build a strong understanding of these advanced SQL concepts. Practicing these questions will equip you to tackle interview challenges, analyze data with precision, and optimize your data manipulation skills. Remember to combine theoretical knowledge with hands-on practice to become proficient in using these powerful SQL features effectively.

CHAPTER 13

Deep Dive

In this section will do a deep dive on popular SQL and Database related interview questions to understand the underlying concept in detail? This list include all kind of SQL questions like SQL query, questions based upon JOIN, Date and Time, and other important SQL Concepts as well questions form MySQL, Oracle, SQL Server, and PostgreSQL

Difference between ROW_NUMBER(), RANK(), and DENSE_RANK()

Though all three are ranking functions in SQL, also known as a window function in Microsoft SQL Server, the difference between `rank()`, `dense_rank()`, and `row_number()` comes when you have ties on ranking i.e. duplicate records.

For example, if you are ranking employees by their salaries then what would be the rank of two employees of the same salaries? It depends on which ranking function you are using like row_number, rank, or dense_rank.

The `row_number()` function always generates a unique ranking even with duplicate records i.e. if the ORDER BY clause cannot distinguish between two rows, it will still give them different rankings, though which record will come earlier or later is decided randomly like in our example two employees Shane and Rick have the same salary and has row number 4 and 5, this is random, if you run again, Shane might come 5th.

The**rank()** and **dense_rank()** will give the same ranking to rows that cannot be distinguished by the order by clause, but dense_rank will always generate a contiguous sequence of ranks like (1,2,3,...), whereas rank() will leave gaps after two or more rows with the same rank (think "Olympic Games": if two athletes win the gold medal, there is no second place, only third).

Surprisingly all these functions behave similarly in Microsoft SQL Server and Oracle, at least at the high level, so if you have used them in MSSQL, you can also use it on Oracle 11g or other versions.

SQL to build schema

Here is the SQL to create a table and insert some data into it for demonstration purpose:

```
IF OBJECT_ID( 'tempdb..#Employee' ) IS NOT NULL
DROP TABLE #Employee;
CREATE TABLE #Employee (name varchar(10), salary int);
INSERT INTO #Employee VALUES ('Rick', 3000);
INSERT INTO #Employee VALUES ('John', 4000);
INSERT INTO #Employee VALUES ('Shane', 3000);
INSERT INTO #Employee VALUES ('Peter', 5000);
INSERT INTO #Employee VALUES ('Jackob', 7000);
INSERT INTO #Employee VALUES ('Sid', 1000);
```

You can see that we have included two employees with the same salaries i.e. Shane and Rick, just to demonstrate the difference between row_number, rank, and dense_rank window function in the SQL server, which is obvious when there are ties in the ranking.

ROW_NUMBER() Example

It always generates a unique value for each row, even if they are the same and the ORDER BY clause cannot distinguish between them. That's why it is used to solve problems like the second-highest salary or nth highest salary, we have seen earlier.

In the following example, we have two employees with the same salary and even though we have generated row numbers over the salary column it produces different row numbers for those two employees with the same salary.

```
select e.*, row_number() over (order by salary desc)
row_number from #Employee e
result:
name      salary   row_number
Jackob    70001
Peter     50002
John      40003
Shane     30004
Rick      30005
Sid       10006
```

You can see in this example that we have ranked employees based upon their salaries and each of them has a unique rank even if their salaries are the same e.g. Shane and Rick have the same salary of 3000 but they got the unique rank 4th and 5th. It's worth knowing that in the case of a tie, ranks are assigned on a random basis.

RANK() Example

The `rank()` function will assign the same rank to the same values i.e. which are not distinguishable by ORDER BY. Also, the next different rank will not start from immediately next number but there will be a gap i.e. if 4th and 5th employees have the same salary then they will have the same rank 4, and 6th employee which has a different salary will have a new rank 6.

Here is the example to clarify the point:

```
select e.*, rank() over (order by salary desc) rank from
#Employee e
result:
name      salary   rank
Jackob    70001
Peter     50002
John      40003
Shane     30004
Rick      30004
Sid       10006
```

You can see that both Shane and Rick have got the same rank 4th, but the Sid got the rank 6th, instead of 5 because it keeps the original ordering.

DENSE_RANK() Example

The dense_rank function is similar to the `rank()` window function i.e. same values will be assigned the same rank, but the next different value will have a rank which is just one more than the previous rank, i.e. if 4th and 5th employee has the same salary then they will have the same rank but 6th employee, which has different salary will have rank 5, unlike rank 6 as is the case with `rank()` function. There will be no gap in ranking in the case of `dense_rank()` as shown in the following example:

```
select e.*, dense_rank() over (order by salary desc)
dense_rank from #Employee e
name      salary  dense_rank
Jackob    70001
Peter     50002
John      40003
Shane     30004
Rick      30004
Sid       10005
```

You can see that both Shane and Rick have the same ranking 4th, but Sid now has 5th rank which is different than 6th in the earlier example when we used the `rank()` function.

Difference between row_number vs rank vs dense_rank

As I told, the **difference between rank, row_number, and dense_rank is visible when there are duplicate records**. Since in all our example we are ranking records on salary, if two records will have the same salary then you will notice the difference between these three ranking functions.

The row_number gives continuous numbers, while rank and dense_rank give the same rank for duplicates, but the next number in rank is as per continuous order so you will see a jump but in dense_rank doesn't have any gap in rankings.

```
-- difference between row_number(), rank(), and
dense_rank()
-- will only visible when there were duplicates.
-- row_number gives consecutive ranking even with
duplicate
-- rank and dense_rank give the same ranking but rank has
a jump
-- while dense_rank doesn't have jump
select e.*,
row_number() over (order by salary desc) row_number,
rank() over (order by salary desc) rank,
dense_rank() over (order by salary desc) as dense_rank
from #Employee e
```

And here is the output which clearly shows the difference in the ranking generated by rank() and dense_rank() function. This will clear your doubt about rank, desnse_rank, and row_nubmer function.

You can see the employees Shane and Rick have the same salary 3000 hence their ranking is the same when you use the rank() and dense_rank() but the next ranking is 6 which is as per continuous ranking using rank() and 5 when you use dense_rank(). The row_number() doesn't break ties and always gives a unique number to each record.

Btw, I ran all three SQL queries on Oracle 11g R2 and, Oracle 12c and it gave me the same result. So, it seems both Oracle and SQL Server support these functions and they behave identically.

That's all about the **difference between ROW_NUMBER(), RANK(), and DENSE_RANK() function in SQL SERVER.** As I told, the difference boils down to the fact when ties happen. In the case of the tie, ROW_NUMBER() will give unique row numbers, the rank will give the same rank, but the next different rank will not be in sequence, there will be a gap.

In the case of dense_rank, both rows in the tie will have the same rank and there will be no gap. The next different rank will be in sequence.

Difference between VARCHAR and NVARCHAR in SQL Server?

There is a subtle difference between these two character data types in SQL Server, while both supports variable length, the VARCHAR data type is used to store non-Unicode characters while NVARCHAR is used to store Unicode characters. It also takes more space than VARCHAR.

For example, in the case of VARCHAR, each character takes 1 byte but in the case of NVARCHAR, each character takes 2 bytes of storage, which means NVARACHAR is twice as expensive as VARCHAR type.

While we will look into the difference between these two, it's also worth noting the similarities between them. For example, both VARCHAR and NVARCHAR are character data types and used to store text or String values. Both are also variable-length data types, so storage size depending upon actual data stored.

Here are a few important differences between VARCHAR and NVARCHAR data types in SQL Server. You can keep these differences in mind while choosing the right data type for your columns in a table or database.

1. VARCHAR is a non-Unicode character data type with a maximum length of 8,000 characters, while NVARCHAR is a Unicode character data type with a maximum length of 4,000 characters.

2. VARCHAR literals are enclosed in single quotes, like 'John,' but NVARCHAR literals are prefixed with N also, for example, N'John.'

3. In the case of VARCHAR data type, each character occupies 1 byte, while in the case of NVARCHAR, each

character needs 2 bytes of storage, which means NVARCHAR is twice as expensive as VARCHAR.

4. Use of index can fail if you provide wrong data type, like in SQL Server, when you have an index over a VARCHAR column and present it a Unicode String, MSSQL Server will not use the index.

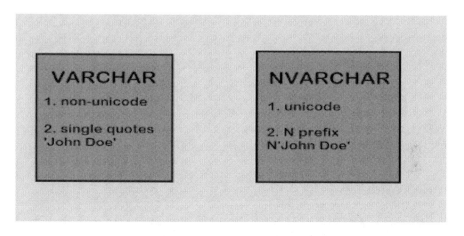

That's all about the difference between VARCHAR and NVARCHAR data types in SQL. You should always use the data type that will take less space. In SQL Server NVARCHAR takes more space than VARCHAR data type, almost 2x as much space as VARCHAR.

You should use VARCHAR if you know that all your data would be in ASCII encoding, but if you are going to store Unicode string, like storing data from different languages. You need to use NVARCHAR to support Unicode data. NVARCHAR is a must if you intend to support internationalization (i18n)

What is difference between SQL, T-SQL and PL/SQL?

Today, we are going to see another common and interesting SQL interview question, **what is the difference between SQL, T-SQL, and PL/SQL?** It is also one of the most common doubts among SQL beginners. It's common for programmers to think that why there are many types of SQL languages, why not just single SQL across DB? etc.

Well, let's first understand the difference between SQL, T-SQL, and PL/SQL, and then we will understand the need for these dialects. SQL is standard for querying, inserting, and modifying data in a relational database. It is categorized into DDL and DML and is powerful enough to create database objects e.g. table, view, stored procedure, and can perform CRUD operation (<u>SELECT</u>, INSERT, UPDATE, and <u>DELETE</u>) query.

On the other hand, **T-SQL** (Transact-SQL) is a dialect used by Microsoft SQL Server and Sybase. It is an extension of SQL and provides more functionality than SQL but at the same time confirming ANSI SQL standard as well. For example, you can use conditionals and loops in T-SQL to create a more sophisticated stored procedure that is not available in standard SQL.

Similarly, **PL/SQL** (Procedural language SEQUEL) is a dialect for Oracle database, which provides T-SQL like functionality e.g. conditionals, loops, and other elements for procedural programming. Both T-SQL and PL/SQL are the supersets of SQL because they not just confirm ANSI SQL standard but also provide additional functionality that is not available in the ANSI standard but helps a lot in database programming.

In this article, we will see a couple of more differences between SQL, T-SQL, and PL/SQL to understand them better.

Why do you need T-SQL or PL/SQL?

Though standard SQL is enough for inserting, retrieving, and modifying data from the database, they only provide set-based operations, which means there are a lot of tasks that you cannot do using plain SQL.

In order to make SQL more powerful and to expand its usage from simple querying to create complex stored procedures for report generation, <u>XSLT transformation</u>, and many other functionalities, various database vendors started adding proprietary features on

SQL supported by their platform. These efforts created different SQL dialects e.g. T-SQL, which is a SQL dialect for Microsoft SQL Server, and Sybase, PL/SQL which is a SQL dialect for Oracle.

In fact, every database has its own SQL dialect, which comprises features and keywords only supported in their database e.g. MySQL has the LIMIT keyword which can be used for pagination or solving problems like <u>second highest salary</u>, but it will not work on Oracle or Microsoft SQL Server database. Similarly, PostgreSQL has some features which are not available to other databases.

It's always recommended to use standard ANSI SQL if it serves your purpose because query written in ANSI SQL is portable across different database vendors but if you use a proprietary keyword e.g. TOP in Microsoft SQL Server, LIMIT in MySQL then you need to change your query when your application migrate from one database to another.

Differences between SQL, T-SQL and PL/SQL

Here are a couple of more differences between SQL, PL/SQL, and T-SQL for interviews:

1. Full form

SQL stands for Structured Query language, T-SQL stands for Transact-SQL and PL/SQL stands for Procedural Language/SQL.

2. Supported Database

SQL is supported across all database vendors like Oracle, SQL Server, MySQL, PostgreSQL, IBM DB2, and even lightweight databases like SQLLite, but T-SQL is only supported in Microsoft SQL Server and Sybase, and PL/SQL is supported only in Oracle.

3. Performance

Another key difference between SQL and PL/SQL, T-SQL is the performance improvement by saving database roundtrip. Both

PL/SQL and T-SQL allow grouping of SQL statements which means if your code has 4 SELECT SQL queries then instead of making four round trips to the database, they can be sent as one single unit to the database and their result will also come back as one unit.

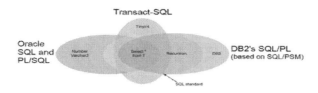

4. SQL Query Requirement

There is an interesting difference between SQL and T-SQL in terms of minimum SELECT query requirements. According to standard SQL, a SELECT query must have at minimum FROM and SELECT clauses, but you can create a SELECT query in T-SQL with just a SELECT clause, without FROM clause. For example, the following SQL query is *invalid* according to SQL standard but it works fine in T-SQL supported databases like Sybase and MSSQL:

```
SELECT 'Java' AS Language, 1 AS RANK;
```

The output of the query is a single row with attributes resulting from the expression with names assigned using the aliases e.g.

Language Rank

Java   1

5. Data Types and Keyword

There are some data types which are supported only by PL/SQL and T-SQL e.g. TINYINT data type is only available in T-SQL and VARCHAR2 and NUMBER is only available in PL/SQL or Oracle database. Similarly, there are keywords which are only

210

available in a particular SQL dialect like the LIMIT keyword which is only available in MySQL.

That's all on the **difference between SQL, T-SQL, and PL/SQL**. Just remember that both T-SQL and PL/SQL are dialects of SQL, which is the standard specified by ANSI for managing data in relational databases. T-SQL is only supported in Sybase and SQL SERVER, while PL/SQL is only supported in the Oracle database. Though both T-SQL and PL/SQL are more powerful than SQL and provide several languages construct to do more with database e.g. conditionals, loops, branching, etc.

How to check for Null in SQL Query?

One of the most common SQL Interview questions on Programming interviews is to select some rows from a table that also contains null values. Since many SQL developers are used to using = and ! = operator on WHERE clause, they often tend to forget the fact that column allows NULL or not.

Using = or != is perfectly fine if your column has NOT NULL constraint and you know for sure that there are no NULL values in that column, but it does contain NULLs then your SQL query will return the incorrect result at times.

This is one of the most common mistakes but at the same time hard to find SQL bugs if it managed to get into the real environment. In this article, you will learn the right way to check NULL values in SQL queries using IS NULL and IS NOT NULL predicates.

The right way to compare values in a column that allows NULL

In most of the SQL interviews, you will be given a table that contains both NULL and non-null values and you need to write some SQL queries to retrieve data from those tables. For example, consider the following table which just contains one column, Id, and the following values.

```
CREATE TABLE #test (id int)
INSERT #test VALUES(1)
INSERT #test VALUES(2)
INSERT #test VALUES(null)
```

Now, the question is, how many records the following query will return?

```
SELECT*FROM#test WHERE id != 1
```

Many SQL programmers will answer that it will return 2 records, which is **wrong**. This query will only return one record, the row with Id=2 as shown below:

```
SELECT*FROM#test WHERE id != 1
id
2
```

Why? Why the row with NULL Id was was not returned? Because when you compare something with NULL the result is **Unknown**, not true or false. SQL uses three value logic, `true`, `false`, and `unknown`.

In order to check for NULL values, you must use **IS NULL** or **IS NOT NULL** clause. For example, to include the row with Id as NULL, you can modify your SQL query like

```
SELECT*FROM#temp WHERE id != 1 OR id IS NULL
Output
id
2
NULL
```

You can see that it returned both rows. Remember even comparing NULL to NULL doesn't work, it also returns unknown e.g. if you try to write the above query using = operator it will not work as shown below:

```
SELECT*FROM#temp WHERE id != 1 OR id = NULL
```

```
id
2
```

You can see it just return 1 row, the row with `Id=NULL` was not included again. Always remember null != null in SQL whether it's Oracle, MySQL, PostgreSQL, or Microsoft SQL Server.

How to test for not null values in SQL? IS NOT NULL Example

Similarly to test for values that are not null, instead of using the ! = operator use IS NOT NULL operator. For example, the following query which we have written to return all the rows where Id is NOT NULL will not work because we are using ! = operator

```
SELECT*FROM#temp WHERE id != NULL
(0 row(s) affected)
```

Instead, you should use **IS NOT NULL** as shown below:

```
SELECT*FROM#temp WHERE id IS NOT NULL
id
1
2
```

That's all about the **right way to check for NULL values in the WHERE clause in the SQL query**. Don't use = or != operator to compare values if your column allows NULLs, it may not return what you expect because comparing NULL with anything else returns Unknown. Instead, you should always use IS NULL and IS NOT NULL to check for null values in SQL queries.

Difference between CAST, CONVERT, and PARSE function in Microsoft SQL Server?

Though all three, CAST, CONVERT, and PARSE are used to convert one data type into another in SQL Server, there are some subtle differences between them. The CAST method accepts just two parameters, expression, and target type, but CONVERT() also takes a **third parameter** representing the format of conversion, which is supported for some conversions, like between character strings and date-time values. For example, CONVERT(DATE, '2/7/2015', 101) converts the character string '2/7/2015' to DATE using DATE format 101, representing United States standard.

By using the PARSE function, you can also indicate the culture by using any culture supported by Microsoft's dot NET framework. For example, PARSE('7/8/2015' AS DATE USING 'en-US') parses the input literal as a DATE by using the United States English Culture, similar to 101 formatting style.

CAST vs CONVERT vs PARSE Exam in SQL Server

Here are some other differences between CAST, CONVERT, and PARSE methods for data type conversion in SQL Server:

1. ANSI SQL Standard

CAST is supported by ANSI SQL Standard, so it's a best practice to prefer CAST over CONVERT and PARSE if it's enough to do the job.

2. .NET and CLR Dependency

PARSE function relies on the presence of the .NET Framework common language runtime (CLR), which may be an extra dependency and may not be present in every Windows server where you have installed Microsoft SQL Server.

3. Optional USING Clause

The PARSE function supports an optional USING clause indicating the culture, which is any valid culture supported by the .NET framework.

If culture is not specified then it will use the current session's effective language.

4. Syntax

Using CAST:

```
CAST ( expression AS data_type )
```

Using CONVERT:

```
CONVERT ( data_type [ ( length ) ] , expression [ ,
style ] )
```

Using PARSE

```
PARSE ( string_value AS data_type [ USING culture ] )
```

Both CAST and CONVERT are used to explicitly converts an expression of different data types in SQL

5. Examples

Let's see some examples to convert DATE to VARCHAR in Microsoft SQL Server using the cast(), convert(), and parse function.

CAST Function Example

Let's some examples of CAST function to convert the <u>DATETIME data type to VARCHAR</u> and VARCHAR data type to SMALLINT data type in SQL Server:

```
-- casting DATE to VARCHAR in SQL Server
SELECT CAST(GETDATE() AS VARCHAR(30)) AS Today
Today
Apr 25 2017 6:32AM
-- CASTING VARCHAR to INT in Microsoft SQL Server
SELECT CAST('1234' AS SMALLINT) AS Number
Number
1234
```

You can see that the casting has been successful.

CONVERT Function Example

Now, let's try to convert the same values using the Convert function in SQL Server:

```
-- converting DATE to VARCHAR in SQL Server
SELECT CONVERT(VARCHAR(20), GETDATE(), 101) AS Today
Today
07/23/2015
-- converting VARCHAR to INT in Microsoft SQL Server
SELECT Convert(bigint, '222222') AS MagicNumber
MagicNumber
222222
```

Convert function is mainly used to convert Date to VARCHAR value into different date formats as shown <u>here</u>.

Here is the screenshot of executing SQL queries with CAST and Convert in SQL Server Management Studio:

216

```
-- converting DATE to VARCHAR in SQL Server
SELECT CONVERT(VARCHAR(20), GETDATE(), 101) AS Today

-- converting VARCHAR to INT in Microsoft SQL Server
SELECT Convert(bigint, '222222') AS MagicNumber

-- casting DATE to VARCHAR in SQL Server
SELECT CAST(GETDATE() AS VARCHAR(30)) AS Today

-- CASTING VARCHAR to INT in Microsoft SQL Server
SELECT CAST('1234' AS SMALLINT) AS Number
```

Today
04/25/2017

MagicNumb...
222222

Today
Apr 25 2017 11:32PM

Number
1234

PARSE Function Example

Let's see some examples of PARSE function to convert VARCHAR data type to DATETIME2 and MONEY data type using different locale or cultures:

```
-- Parsing VARCHAR to DATETIME2 data type
SELECT PARSE('Monday, 25 December 2017' AS datetime2
      USING 'en-US') AS CurrentDate;
CurrentDate
2017-12-25 00:00:00.0000000
-- Parsing VARCHAR with currency symbol to MONEY data
type
SELECT PARSE('€345,98' AS money USING 'de-DE') AS Price;
Price
345.98
```

You can see that the amount of currency value Euro is parsed correctly because of German culture, but if you try to change the currency symbol to $ it will not parse and give you an error as shown below:

```
-- Parsing VARCHAR with dollar currency symbol to MONEY
data type
--- using german culture
SELECT PARSE('$345,98' AS money USING 'de-DE') AS Price;
Msg 9819, Level 16, State 1, Line 2
Error converting string value '$345,98' into data type
money
using culture 'de-DE'.
```

217

But as soon as you change the culture to `en-US` it will be able to parse the currency value correctly, but do note down the actual value which is very different from the german one, that's where culture can make a big difference.

```
-- Parsing VARCHAR with dollar currency symbol to MONEY
data type
--- using US culture
SELECT PARSE('$345,98' AS money USING 'en-US') AS Price;
Price
34598.00
```

Here is one more example of using the PARSE function in SQL Server to parse String using implicit language setting

```
-- PARSE with implicit setting of language
-- The English language is mapped to en-US specific
culture
SET LANGUAGE 'English';
SELECT PARSE('04/16/2017' AS datetime2) AS Output;
Output
2017-04-16 00:00:00.0000000
```

Here is the screenshot of executing PARSE related SQL queries on the SSMS tool:

That's all about the **difference between CAST, CONVERT, and PARSE in SQL SERVER**. Prefer CAST over CONVERT and PARSE because it's ANSI standard and your query will be more portable across different database vendors. I generally prefer CAST for casting between VARCHAR and NUMERIC type, but I prefer to use CONVERT for converting String literals into DATE, TIME, and DATETIME types. I don't use PARSE, but it is something good to know about it.

Difference between UNION vs UNION ALL in SQL

Hello guys, what is the difference between UNION vs UNION ALL is one of the most popular SQL interview questions and often asked programmers during a telephonic round of interviews. Though both UNION and UNION ALL is used to combine results of two SELECT queries, the main difference between them is that **UNION doesn't include duplicate record** but **UNION ALL does**.

Another difference between them is that UNION ALL is faster than UNION but may look slow because it returns more data which takes more time to travel via the network. The difference between UNION and UNION ALL can be a tricky SQL question, especially for developers, who have not used this useful keyword ever.

Since the UNION clause is not as common as a SELECT clause in SQL, it's usually asked in a telephonic round of programming interviews to check whether the candidate is comfortable with SQL or not. It's in the same league of questions like clustered vs non-clustered index or primary vs unique key. UNION is very different than other SQL commands because it operates on data rather than columns.

Anyway, the answer to this question is simple, though both UNION and UNION ALL are used to combine the result of two separate SQL queries on the same or different table, UNION does not keep a duplicate record (a row is considered duplicate if the value of all columns is same), while UNION ALL does.

Since you mostly **don't want duplicate rows**, UNION is preferred over UNION ALL in reporting and application development. By the way, you should keep in mind that UNION ALL performance better than UNION because it doesn't have to remove duplicates, so no extra work.

This keyword is very well supported by all major databases like Oracle, Microsoft SQL Server, MySQL, and PostgreSQL. Another thing to keep in mind is the amount of data returned by UNION ALL; if your database server is quite far away and you have limited bandwidth, UNION ALL may appear slower than UNION because of the number of duplicates it returned.

The cost of transferring duplicate rows can exceed the query execution benefits in many cases. We will see a couple of *examples UNION and UNION ALL in SQL*, but before that few things to keep in mind. In order to combine the results of two queries, they must contain the same number of columns.

For example, if one query contains 3 columns and the other contains 4 columns then you cannot use UNION or UNION ALL. This is because a row will only be considered duplicated when all columns will have the same value, irrespective of the name of the columns themselves.

UNION and UNION ALL Example in Microsoft SQL Server

Let's see one simple example of UNION and UNION ALL, this will not only show you how they work but also where you can use them. This example is from my sample database and the following screenshot is from SQL Server Management Studio.

We have two tables, Employee and Customer. In order to use UNION and UNION ALL, I have kept the same persons as employee and customer, so you will see the same id on emp_id and customer_id, and the same name as well.

If you look at the result of the first two select queries, you will see that the first query returns two rows and the second query returns three rows, where two rows have exactly the same data as the first query.

Key things to note is that column names are different in both result sets, first one has `emp_id` and `emp_name`, while second data set has `customer_id` and `customer_name`, but most important both dataset has only two columns. This is a must in order to combine them using `UNION` and `UNION ALL` keywords.

The third query is an example of how to use the *UNION clause in SQL*, you can see that the combined result has just three columns, all are <u>unique</u>. Duplicate columns from the second result set were not included. This is more like how you do `UNION` in Set theory, where the final result contains data from both sets.

The fourth query is how you should use `UNION ALL`, it contains five rows, two from the first query and three from the second query. It has not removed duplicate rows from the second query, that's why you see `Ken` and `Bob` repeating twice.

This example teaches us the core concept that the `UNION` doesn't depend upon the column name but the data. You can combine the result of as many queries as possible until the number of columns in all of them is the same and the data is from the same set.

Regarding performance, you need to run `UNION` and `UNION ALL` with a large database, containing millions of rows. There you can monitor how much time both takes and compare them.

Theoretically, `UNION ALL` should take less time to execute but more time to transfer data to the client.

```sql
select emp_id, emp_name from Employee

select customer_id, customer_name from Customer

select emp_id, emp_name from Employee
UNION
select customer_id, customer_name from Customer

select emp_id, emp_name from Employee
UNION ALL
select customer_id, customer_name from Customer
```

100 % ▾

▦ Results 🔲 Messages

	emp_id	emp_na...
1	101	Ken
2	201	Bob

	customer...	customer_na...
1	101	Ken
2	201	Bob
3	211	Ragho

	emp_id	emp_na...
1	101	Ken
2	201	Bob
3	211	Ragho

	emp_id	emp_na...
1	101	Ken
2	201	Bob
3	101	Ken
4	201	Bob
5	211	Ragho

Difference between UNION and UNION ALL command in SQL

Now we know how union and union all works and has some background by following the above examples, let's summarise the similarities and difference between them for quick revision :

1. Combining Results

Both UNION and UNION ALL are used to combine the results of two separate SQL queries, it could be on the same table or a different table but the data should be the same.

For example, if product_id is used in two tables like Product and Order, then two SQL queries which pulls product_id from these two tables can be combined using UNION or UNION ALL.

2. Duplicates

The key difference between UNION and UNION ALL is that the former will remove duplicates but later will keep them. In other words, UNION is equal to running distinct on the output of UNION ALL.

For example, if product_id 10 is returned by both SQL query then it will only appear once if you use UNION and appear twice if you use UNION ALL.

3. Execution time

Due to the above difference query execution time of UNION ALL is smaller than UNION, which means the former runs faster than the latter. So if you want faster output and don't care about duplicates use UNION ALL.

This is something you can also guess from your existing SQL knowledge and that's where working on fundamentals pays off.

4. Speed and Bandwith Usage

You should keep in mind that benefits gained by not removing duplicates can be easily wiped out by transferring more data over a poor bandwidth network connection.

That's why in practice some time `UNION ALL` *appears slower than* `UNION` because it returns a lot of data with duplicates which require more time to travel from database server to client machine. To evaluate the performance of `UNION` and `UNION ALL` case by case.

5. Number of Columsn on ResultSet

Another worth noting thing while using `UNION` and `UNION ALL` is that all queries combined using a `UNION, INTERSECT,` or `EXCEPT` operator must have an equal number of expressions in their target lists.

For example, if the result of query 1 has three columns and the result of query 2 has two columns then you cannot combine them using the `UNION` command.

That's all on the **difference between the UNION and UNION ALL command in SQL**. It's one of the useful commands to combine the result of two `SELECT` queries when they contain the same data. There are many practical scenarios where `UNION` is very useful, for example when you need to create a list out of different tables containing data from the same set.

The main *difference between UNION and UNION ALL is about duplicates*, the former removes it while later keeps it, other differences between them on performance and networking bandwidth usage can be easily derived by knowing this difference. Also keep in mind that it is well supported big three databases like MySQL, Oracle, and SQL Server. Let us know if you have been asked this question in your SQL interview.

Difference between table scan, index scan, and index seek in SQL Server Database

Hello guys, a good understanding of how the index works and how to use them to improve your SQL query performance is very important while working in a database and SQL and that's why you will find many questions based upon indexes on Programming Job interviews. One of such frequently asked SQL questions is the real *difference between table scan, index scan, and index seek?* Which one is faster and why?

How the database does chooses which scan or seek to use? And how you can optimize the performance of your <u>SQL SELECT queries</u> by using this knowledge. In general, there are only two ways in which your query engine retrieves the data, using a **table scan** or by using an **index**.

Which method is used for your particular query depends upon what indexes are available in that table, what columns you are requesting in your query, the kind of joins you are doing, and the size of your tables.

If you have a clear understanding of how the index works and how the SQL engine retrieves data from the disk then you can quickly identify performance problems and solve them. That's where most of the SQL developers, especially the Java application developer who write queries and design databases lack.

Btw, if you are not familiar with what is an index and how to create and drop an index, then I suggest you first go through these <u>free SQL and Database courses</u> to learn those basics.

Difference between table scan, index scan, and index seek in Database

In this article, we'll go through each three i.e. table scan, index scan, and index seek, and try to understand how databases process a particular query hence a basic understanding of database, SQL and index is required.

1. What is a Table Scan in a database?

A table scan is a pretty straightforward process. When your query engine performs a table scan it starts from the physical beginning of the table and goes through every row in the table. If a row matches the criterion then it includes that into the result set.

You might have heard nasty things about table scans but in truth, it's the fastest way to retrieve data especially if your table is quite small. It starts being bad when your table starts growing. You can imagine doing a full table scan in a table with **4 million rows** and a full table scan in a table with just 100 rows.

In a small table, a query engine can load all data in just one shot but in a large table, it's not possible, which means more IO and more time to process those data.

Normally, a *full table scan* is used when your query doesn't have a WHERE clause, I mean, you want more or less every record from a table like the following query will use a full table scan:

```
SELECT * from Employee;
```

Btw, if your query is taking too long in a large table then most likely it using either table scan or index scan. You can see that by enabling an execution plan like by doing **Ctrl + A** in Microsoft SQL Server Management Studio

2. What is the Index Scan in a database?

If your table has a clustered index and you are firing a query that needs all or most of the rows i.e. query without WHERE or HAVING clause, then it uses an index scan. It works similar to the table scan, during the query optimization process, the query optimizer takes a look at the available index and chooses the best one, based on information provided in your joins and where clause, along with the statistical information database keeps.

Once the right index is chosen, the SQL Query processor or engine navigates the tree structure to the point of data that matches your criteria and again extracts only the records it needs

The *main difference between a full table scan and an index scan* is that because data is sorted in the index tree, the query engine knows when it has reached the end of the current it is looking for. It can then send the query, or move on to the next range of data as necessary.

For example, the following query, same as above will use Index scan if you have a <u>clustered index</u> in your table:

```
SELECT * From Employee;
```

This is slightly faster than the table scan but considerably slower than an index seek which we'll see in the next section.

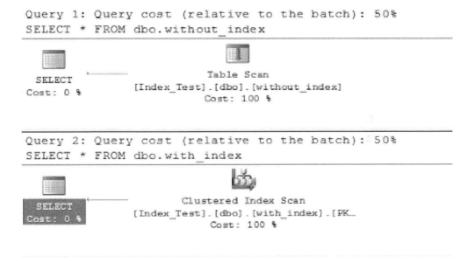

Query 1: Query cost (relative to the batch): 50%
SELECT * FROM dbo.without_index

SELECT
Cost: 0 %

Table Scan
[Index_Test].[dbo].[without_index]
Cost: 100 %

Query 2: Query cost (relative to the batch): 50%
SELECT * FROM dbo.with_index

SELECT
Cost: 0 %

Clustered Index Scan
[Index_Test].[dbo].[with_index].[PK...
Cost: 100 %

3. What is Index Seek in SQL?

When your search criterion matches an index well enough that the index can navigate directly to a particular point in your data, that's called an *index seek*. It is the fastest way to retrieve data in a database. The index seeks are also a great sign that your indexes are being properly used.

This happens when you specify a condition in <u>WHERE</u> clause like searching an employee by id or name if you have a respective index.

For example, the following query will use an index seek, you can also confirm that by checking the execution plan of this query when you run this on SQL server:

```
SELECT * from Employee where EmployeeId=3;
```

In this case, the Query Optimizer can use an index to directly go to the third employee and retrieve the data. If you look at the execution plan shown below, you can see that it uses an index seek using the index created on `EmployeeId`.

Difference between table scan, index scan, and index seek in SQL

Based upon our understanding of indexes, you can now deduce the following points to summarize the difference between table scan, index scan, and index seek in a database:

1. A **table scan** and an **index scan** are used when you need to retrieve all data like 90% to 100% while index seek is used when you need to retrieve data based upon some conditions like 10% of data.

2. If your query doesn't have a WHERE clause and your table doesn't have a clustered index then a full table scan is used, if it does have a <u>clustered index</u> then an index scan is used.

3. Index scan is faster than a table scan because they look at sorted data and query optimizers know when to stop and look for another range.

4. Index seek is the fastest way to retrieve data and it comes into the picture when your search criterion is very specific. Normally, when you have a WHERE clause in your query and you are using a column that also has an index, then index seek is used to retrieve data as shown in the following query:

```
select * from Employee whereId= 3;
```

You can confirm that by actually looking at the execution plan for your query.

In MSSQL management studio, you can see the execution plan by clicking **Ctrl + A** and then running your query.

That's all about the **difference between table scan, index scan and index seek in a database**. As I told you, there are only two ways to retrieve data in a database either by using a table scan or by using an index. The latter is faster in the case of large tables. The choice of the index depends upon multiple things like the WHERE clause and joins in your table, the columns you are requesting, the size of tables, etc.

If you feel that your query is slow, you must check the execution plan to confirm whether it's using index seeks or index scan, or table scan. Then you can optimize your query by introducing the right index or tuning your query.

Difference between ISNULL() and COALESCE() function in SQL?

Even though both ISNULL() and COALESCE() function provides alternate values to NULL in T-SQL and Microsoft SQL Server e.g. replacing NULL values with empty String, there are some key differences between them, which is often the topic of SQL Server interview. In this article, you will not only learn the answer to this question but also learn how to use COALESCE and ISNULL function properly. One of the main differences between them is that COALESCE() is a standard SQL function but ISNULL() is Microsoft SQL Server-specific, which means it's not guaranteed to be supported by other database vendors like Oracle, MySQL, or PostgreSQL.

But, perhaps the most important difference between them is that COALESCE is more flexible and powerful than ISNULL().

229

With `ISNULL()`, you can only provide one alternate value but with COALESCE you can provide more than one e.g. if col1 IS NULL then take value from column2, if that is NULL then take the default value.

Btw, that's not the only difference, there are three key differences between ISNULL() and COALESCE() which we will explore in this article.

Difference between ISNULL() vs COALESCE() in SQL Server

There are three major differences between these two functions besides being ANSI standard or not:

1. COALESCE correctly promotes its arguments to the highest data type in the expression list, but ISNULL doesn't.
2. COALESCE is more flexible and allows you to provide multiple columns and default values but ISNULL can only work with two values.
3. In the case of ISNULL, the alternate value takes the length of the first value but this doesn't happen in the case of COALESCE. This means the type of COALESCE expression is determined by the returned element whereas the return type of ISNULL is determined by the first input.
4. When you use them in a SELECT INTO query then both will produce a NON-NULL value in the result table if the attribute has NON NULL constraint but if it doesn't then COALESCE will create an attribute that allows <u>NULL</u> and ISNULL will create which doesn't allow NULLs

Now let's understand each point in little more detail.

1. COALESCE promotes its argument to the higher data type.

As I have said before that, COALESCE correctly promotes its arguments to the highest data type in the expression list, while ISNULL just looks at the data type of the first argument and makes everything of that type. Let's see an SQL query to understand this point:

```
SELECT 19 / ISNULL(CONVERT(INT,NULL), 3.00);
Output
6
SELECT 19 / COALESCE(CONVERT(INT,NULL), 3.00)
Output
6.333333
```

In the first SQL query, we have used ISNULL and the first data type is INT but because of its NULL, it also converts 3.00 to INT and performed integer arithmetic, but COALESCE correctly promotes the 19 to FLOAT and performed floating-point arithmetic.

2. COALESCE allows multiple values but ISNULL allows only one value

You can provide COALESCE multiple values to use in case the target is NULL.

For example, in the following query, we have provided four options to COALESCE

```
DECLARE @x VARCHAR(10)
DECLARE @y VARCHAR(10)
DECLARE @z VARCHAR(10)
DECLARE @a VARCHAR(10)
SELECT @a = 'SQL'
--This will return SQL
SELECT COALESCE(@x,@y,@z,@a)
Output
SQL
With ISNULL, you can only provide two values e.g.
SELECT ISNULL(@x,@y); --NULL
SELECT ISNULL(@x,@a); --SQL
```

This flexibility allows you to replace complex case statements with simple coalesce functions called on SQL Server stored procedures and functions. See these <u>free SQL and database courses</u> to learn more about it.

3. Length of Result

In the case of COALESCE data type of the result, value determines the type of COALESCE expression but in the case of ISNULL, it's the type of the first argument. For example, see the following T-SQL Query:

```
DECLARE
@a AS VARCHAR(4) = NULL,
@b AS VARCHAR(10) = '1234567890';
SELECT COALESCE(@a, @b) AS [COALESCE], ISNULL(@a, @b) AS
[ISNULL];
Output
COALESCE ISNULL
1234567890 1234
```

You can see that in the case of COALESCE() the result has type and length VARCHAR(10) but in the case of ISNULL() is the length of the first value i.e. length is 4 characters. Another worth noting thing is the use of square bracket e.g. [ISNULL], we do this when we use any keyword or function as literal i.e. variable name or column name.

4. The behavior of COALESCE and ISNULL when used in SELECT INTO

One more difference between COALESCE and ISNULL comes when you are using them in the SELECT INTO clause. If you don't know you can create a table by copying data and schema from another table by using the SELECT INTO clause.

If you are using something like:

```
COALESCE(column1, 0) as new_column
```

vs

```
ISNULL(column1, 0) as new_column.
```

Then, both expressions will produce a NOT NULL attribute in result table if the source is defined as NOT NULL, but in case source attribute allows NULLs then COALESCE will create an attribute that allows <u>NULL</u> and ISNULL will create which doesn't allow NULLs.

That's all about the **difference between ISNULL and COALESCE in SQL Server**. Generally, it's recommended to stick to standard features unless there is some flexibility or major performance you get by using a non-standard feature.

Since ISNULL is actually more limited than COALESCE, so there is no reason to use ISNULL over COALESCE, unless you find ISNULL more readable than COALESCE, like many beginners.

Btw, you must remember these key differences between ISNULL and COALESCE if you are refactoring code and replacing ISNULL with COALESCE in your SQL Script.

How to Find Nth Highest Salary in MySQL and SQL Server? Example LeetCode Solution

Nth Highest Salary in MySQL and SQL Server - LeetCode Solution

Write a SQL query to get the nth highest salary from the Employee table.

```
+----+--------+
| Id | Salary |
+----+--------+
| 1  | 100    |
| 2  | 200    |
| 3  | 300    |
+----+--------+
```

For example, given the above Employee table, the nth highest salary where n = 2 is 200. If there is no nth highest salary, then the query should return `null`.

1. Accepted Solution

This was my accepted solution for this LeetCode problem:

```
CREATE FUNCTION getNthHighestSalary(N INT) RETURNS INT
BEGIN
DECLARE M INT;
SET M = N - 1;
RETURN (
     # WRITE your MySQL query statement below.
SELECT DISTINCT Salary FROM Employee ORDER BY Salary DESC
LIMIT M, 1
);
END
```

2. Alternate Solution

This is another solution to **find Nth highest salary problem**, this was not accepted by LeetCode compiler but they work fine on Database

```
CREATE FUNCTION getNthHighestSalary(N INT) RETURNS INT
BEGIN
RETURN (
     # WRITE your MySQL query statement below.
SELECT Salary FROM Employee a
            WHERE N = (SELECT COUNT(Salary)
                       FROM Employee b
WHERE a.Salary &lt;= b.Salary)
);
END
```

3. How to create own Employee table for testing?

If you want to test in your local database then you can use the following SQL query to create an Employee table and populate with some sample data. After that, you can run the SQL query to find the Nth highest salary for testing.

```
CREATE TABLE Employee (
   Id INT NOT NULL,
   Salary INT NULL
);
INSERT INTO Employee VALUES (1, 100);
INSERT INTO Employee VALUES (2, 200);
INSERT INTO Employee VALUES (3, 300);
```

4. SQL query to find the Nth highest salary

Here is the SQL query you can use to find the Nth highest salary for the above table, you can run this in your local database and it should return the

```
SELECT Salary FROM Employee  a
WHERE N = ( SELECT COUNT(Salary) FROM Employee b WHERE
a.Salary &lt;= b.Salary );
```

For example, given the above Employee table, the nth highest salary where n = 2 is 200. If there is no Nth highest salary, then the query should return `null`. You can see that we have used the above query to find the highest, **second-highest**, and **third-highest salaries** from the employee table.

Difference between VARCHAR and CHAR data type in SQL Server?

Hello all, today, I am going to share an interesting SQL Server interview question, which will not only help you in your interview but also in your day-to-day work. It explains one of the critical concepts of SQL Server, the **difference between VARCHAR and CHAR data type**. I am sure, you all have used both of them numerous times but because it's so common many of us ignore the difference between them and when asked to choose between VARCHAR and CHAR on interviews, they fail to give a convincing reason. The difference is not just significant from an interview point of view but also from a robust database design because an incorrect choice of data type not only limit what kind of data you can put on but also waste precious space and makes your query slower, particularly when you have to deal with the massive amount of data.

In order to understand the difference, it's also essential to understand the similarity between them so, let's start with that. VARCHAR and CHAR both stores character, text, or String data like name, address, etc. One of the important detail to know here is that both stores non-Unicode characters, and there is a separate data type NCHAR and NVARCHAR for storing Unicode characters.

The key difference between CHAR and VARCHAR is that the former is a fixed-length data type while later is a variable-length data type. Yes, the VAR stands for variable length in VARCHAR. To give you an example, CHAR(10) is a fixed-length non-Unicode string of length 10, while VARCHAR(10) is a variable-length non-Unicode string with a maximum length of 10.

This means the actual length will depend upon the data. For example, if you are going to sore a single character string like "Y" then VARCHAR will take less space than CHAR because it will adjust depending upon the length of data. Typically, you would use the char if all data values are 10 characters and varchar if the lengths vary.

It's better to use the data type that will take less space. In SQL Server 2005, 2008, 2012, and 2014, NVARCHAR takes more space than VARCHAR data type, almost 2x as much space as VARCHAR.

So, use VARCHAR if you know that all your data would be in ASCII encoding, but if you are going to store Unicode strings like storing data from different languages, then you need to use NVARCHAR to support Unicode data.

NVARCHAR is a must if you intend to support internationalization (i18n)

Similarities between CHAR vs. VARCHAR in SQL

Now, that you understand the fundamental similarity and differences between char and varchar, let's see some more important points for revision:

1. Both stores non-Unicode characters.
2. Both are character data types.

3. Both take 1 byte to store one character.

4. The maximum length of both CHAR and VARCHAR data types is 8000 characters in SQL Server. Maximum length is defined in parenthesis, e.g. maximum length of CHAR(6) is 6 characters, and the maximum length of VARCHAR(6) is also 6 characters.

The size (9000) given to the type 'varchar' exceeds the maximum allowed for any data type (8000).

```
DECLARE @abc ASCHAR (8000);
DECLARE @abcd ASVARCHAR (8000);
```

Don't confuse length and size here, the length here represents how many characters a CHAR or VARCHAR variable can take, and size represents the storage bytes they take to store those characters.

CHAR vs. VARCHAR in SQL Server

And, here are some of the key differences between CHAR and VARCHAR data types in SQL

1. Fixed vs Variable storage

CHAR is a fixed storage data type, but VARCHAR is a variable storage data type.

What this means is that the storage size of the CHAR column or variable is always fixed, as specified initially but the storage size of the VARCHAR column or variable depends upon actually stored data.

For example, if you create a variable of type CHAR(6) then it will always take 6 bytes, whether or not you store six characters (1 byte per character) but VARCHAR(6) column can take anything between 2 to 8 bytes. 2 bytes are additional overhead, and 1 to 6 bytes are actual storage depending upon how many characters you store.

2.Usage

You should use CHAR when your data is of fixed length, like telephone numbers, zip code, cc number, ba num, ss numbers, etc.

Another use of CHAR data type is storing boolean columns like 'Y' and 'N'.

You can use the VARCHAR type column to store things that are not of fixed length like name, comment, etc.

3. Storage

CHAR variables always take the same storage space irrespective of the number of characters actually stored, while the VARCHAR variable's storage size depends upon the actual number of characters stored.

4. Space Overhead

VARCHAR data type has an overhead of 2 bytes as compared to CHAR variables. This means if your data is always fixed length, then storing them into VARCHAR will take more space than CHAR.

5. Padding

In the case of CHAR, data are padded to make specific characters long, no padding is done on VARCHAR columns

6. Null

A CHAR column cannot hold a NULL, so behind the scene, SQL will actually use a VARCHAR field like CHAR(x) NULL column is actually a VARCHAR(x) column.

7. Reservation

CHAR reserves storage space, VARCHAR doesn't

Use of index can fail if you provide wrong data type like in SQL Server when you have an index over a VARCHAR column and present it a Unicode String, MSSQL Server will not use the index.

That's all about the **difference between CHAR and VARCHAR data types in SQL**. In short, CHAR is a fixed-size data type, while VARCHAR is a variable-size data type, where actual storage space depends upon an actual number of characters stored in the column.

You should always use the right data type to minimize storage requirements. Using incorrect data types not only results in wasted space but also affects the performance of the SQL query.

Difference between WHERE and HAVING clause in SQL? Example

The main difference between the WHERE and HAVING clauses comes when used together with the GROUP BY clause. In that case, WHERE is used to filter rows before grouping, and HAVING is used to exclude records after grouping. This is the most important difference, and if you remember this, it will help you write better SQL queries. This is also one of the important SQL concepts to understand, not just from an interview perspective but also from a day-to-day use perspective. I am sure you have used the WHERE clause because it's one of the most common clauses in SQL along with SELECT and used to specify filtering criteria or conditions.

You can even use the WHERE clause without HAVING or GROUP BY, as you have seen many times. On the other hand, HAVING can only be used if grouping has been performed using the GROUP BY clause in the SQL query.

Another worth noting thing about the WHERE and HAVING clause is that the WHERE clause cannot contain aggregate functions like COUNT(), SUM(), MAX(), MIN(), etc but the HAVING clause may contain aggregate functions.

Another worth noting the difference between WHERE and HAVING clause is that WHERE is used to impose filtering criterion on a SELECT, UPDATE, DELETE statement as well as single row function and used before group by clause but HAVING is always used after group by clause.

If you are starting with SQL, then these are some of the fundamentals you need to learn, and a good course can help you a lot. If you need a recommendation, I suggest you join any of these **best SQL and database courses** online. This list contains the best courses from Udmey, Coursera, Pluralsight, and other websites.

Difference between WHERE vs. HAVING in SQL

1. WHERE clause is processed right after FROM clause in the logical order of query processing, which means it is processed before GROUP BY clause while HAVING clause is executed after groups are created.

2. If used in <u>GROUP BY</u>, You can refer to any column from a table in the WHERE clause, but you can only use columns that are not grouped or aggregated.

3. If you use the HAVING clause without group by, it can also refer to any column, but the index will not be used as opposed to the WHERE clause. For example, the following have the same result set, however "where" will use the id index and having will do a table scan

```
select * fromtablewhereid = 1
select * from the tablehavingid = 1
```

1. You can use an aggregate function to filter rows with the HAVING clause. Because the HAVING clause is processed after the rows have been grouped, you can refer to an aggregate function in the logical expression. For

240

example, the following query will display only courses which have more than 10 students :

```
SELECT Course, COUNT(Course) as NumOfStudent
FROM Training
GROUP BY Course
HAVINGCOUNT(Course)> 10
```

1. Another key difference between WHERE and HAVING clause is that WHERE will use Index and HAVING will not; for example following two queries will produce an identical result, but WHERE will use Index and HAVING will do a table scan

```
SELECT * FROM Course WHEREId = 101;
SELECT * FROM Course HAVINGId = 102;
```

1. Since the WHERE clause is evaluated before groups are formed, it evaluates for per row. On the other hand, the HAVING clause is evaluated after groups are formed; hence it evaluates per group. You can further see these free SQL online courses to learn more about it.

Sno	Where Clause	Having Clause
1	The WHERE clause specifies the criteria which individual records must meet to be selcted by a query. It can be used without the GROUP BY clause	The HAVING clause cannot be used without the GROUP BY clause.
2	The WHERE clause selects rows before grouping.	The HAVING clause selects rows after grouping.
3	The WHERE clause cannot contain aggregate functions	The HAVING clause can contain aggregate functions.
4	WHERE clause is used to impose condition on SELECT statement as well as single row function and is used before GROUP BY clause	HAVING clause is used to impose condition on GROUP Function and is used after GROUP BY clause in the query
5	SELECT Column,AVG(Column_nmae)FROM Table_name WHERE Column > value GROUP BY Column_nmae	SELECT Columnq, AVG(Column_nmae)FROM Table_name WHERE Column > value GROUP BY Column_nmae Having column_name>or<value

When to use WHERE and HAVING clauses?

Though both are used to exclude rows from the result set, you should use the WHERE clause to filter rows before grouping and use the HAVING clause to filter rows after grouping. In other words, WHERE can be used to filter on table columns while HAVING can be used to filter on aggregate functions like count, sum, avg, min, and max.

If filtering can be done without aggregate function then you must do it on the <u>WHERE clause</u> because it improves performance because counting and sorting will be done on a much smaller set. If you filter the same rows after grouping, you unnecessarily bear the cost of sorting, which is not used.

For example, the following statement is syntactically correct and produce the same result, but the second one is more efficient than the first one because it filters rows before grouping :

```
SELECT Job, City, State, Count(Employee) from ...
HAVING...
SELECT ..... from .. WHERE ..
```

That's all about the **difference between WHERE and HAVING clause in SQL**. These differences are valid for almost all major databases like MySQL, Oracle, SQL Server, and PostgreSQL. Just remember that WHERE is used to filter rows before grouping while HAVING is used to filter rows after grouping. You can also use the AGGREGATE function along with the HAVING clause for filtering.

Difference between Primary key vs Candidate Key in SQL Database?

What is the *difference between primary key and candidate key* is another popular SQL and database interview question which appears in various <u>programming interviews</u> now and then? The concept of primary key and candidate key is not just important from the interview point of view but also in designing databases and normalization.

By the way, this is my second post about primary keys, In the last one, we have seen a comparison of primary key vs unique key, which also happens to be one of the frequently asked database questions.

By definition primary key is a column or collection of columns, which uniquely defines a row in a table. Candidate keys are keys that can be a primary key and also able to uniquely identify any row in the table.

In simple terms, you may have a couple of Candidate keys and you have chosen one of them as a primary key.

This selection part is the most important skill in database design. Since only the primary key can have a clustered index in a table while unique keys can have a Nonclustered index, it's important to choose the right column or collection of columns as a primary key. Often I select a column that is most frequently used in the Where clause of the SELECT query.

Btw, If you are new to SQL and don't understand fundamentals like primary key, normalization, and basic SQL queries then you can also join these free SQL courses to learn those SQL fundamentals. It's one of the best resources to learn SQL online.

Difference between Correlated and Non-Correlated Subquery in SQL

The **correlated subquery** is one of the tricky concepts of SQL. It'2s similar to recursion in programming which many programmers struggle to understand, but like recursion, it also offers the unique capability to solve many SQL query-based problems like the second-highest salary problem where you need to compare one row of the table to another row. It gives you a different kind of power. The main difference between a regular, non-correlated, and correlated subquery in SQL is in their working, a regular subquery just runs once and returns a value or a set of values that is used by the outer query.

While correlated subquery runs for each row returned by the outer query because the output of the whole query is based upon comparing the data returned by one row to all other rows of the table. That's why it is also very slow and generally avoided until you don't know any other way to solve the problem.

One of the most popular examples of the correlated subquery is about finding the second highest salary of an employee in a given table. Even though there are multiple ways to solve this problem like you can use window functions like row_number or rank but using a regular subquery to solve this problem is the easiest way.

Btw, even though you can solve this problem by using a regular query it becomes tricky when the Interviewer extends this problem to find the Nth highest salary then you just can't go with regular subquery because of unlimited nesting.

Correlated subquery solves this problem elegantly as shown here. It compares data returned by an outer query like salary and compares with other salaries to find out exactly how many salaries are higher than this salary.

Difference between Correlated and Regular Subquery in SQL

The difference between correlated and regular subquery is also a frequently asked SQL interview question. Mostly asked on a telephonic interview where they cannot ask you to solve queries and check the fundamentals and theoretical concepts.

In this article, I am going to compare correlated subquery with the regular one of different parameters e.g. their working, speed, performance, and dependency. I'll also give you a good example of a correlated subquery e.g. the Nth highest salary problem and explain how exactly it solves the problem.

So, if the interviewer asks you to find the 4th highest salary then there can only be at most 4 salaries which is equal to or greater than the 4th highest salary. This is just an example, you can use a correlated subquery to solve many such problems in the world of data and SQL. In short, here are the *main difference between correlated and non-correlated subqueries in SQL*

1. Working

A non-correlated subquery is executed only once and its result can be swapped back for a query, on the other hand, **a correlated subquery is executed multiple times**, precisely once for each row returned by the outer query.

For example, the following query is an example of a non-correlated subquery:

```
SELECT MAX(Salary) FROM Employee
WHERE Salary NOT IN ( SELECT MAX(Salary) FROM Employee)
```

Here the subquery is SELECT MAX(Salary) from Employee, you can execute and substitute the result of that query e.g. if subquery return 10000 then the outer query is reduced to

```
SELECT MAX(Salary) from Employee where Salary NOT IN
(10000).
```

This is not possible with a correlated subquery, which needs to be executed multiple times as shown below:

```
SELECT e.Name, e.Salary FROM Employee e
WHERE 2 = (
SELECT COUNT(Salary) FROM Employee p WHERE p.salary >=
e.salary)
```

In this example, the subquery is SELECT COUNT(Salary) FROM Employee p WHERE p.salary >= e.salary, you cannot swap its value for the outer query because it needs to be executed for each employee.

Let's say the first row of employees has a salary of 5000, in this case, e.salary will be 500 and subquery will be

```
SELECT COUNT(Salary) FROM Employee p WHERE p.salary >=
5000
```

and subquery will find how many salaries are higher than 5000 if count return 2 then it's the <u>second-highest salary</u>. This logic needs to be executed for each row the outer query will process.

2. Dependency

A *correlated subquery depends upon the outer query* and *cannot execute in isolation,* but a regular or non-correlated subquery doesn't depend on the outer query and can execute in isolation.

From the above example, you can see that a correlated subquery like SELECT COUNT(Salary) FROM Employee p WHERE p.salary >= e.salary depends upon outer query because it needs the value of e.salary, which comes from the table listed on the outer query.

On the other hand, regular subquery, SELECT MAX(Salary) FROM Employee doesn't depends upon the outer query and can be executed in isolation or independently of the outer query. You can further join these <u>free SQL and database courses</u> to learn more about Correlated and non-correlated subqueries and how to use them.

<u>Co-related</u>

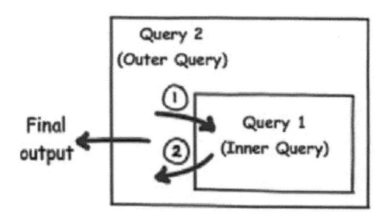

3.Speed and Performance

A **correlated subquery is much slower** than a non-correlated subquery because in the former, the inner query executes for each row of the outer query. This means if your table has n rows then whole processing will take the **n * n = n^2** time, as compared to 2n times taken by a non-correlated subquery.

This happens because to execute a non-correlated subquery you need to examine just n rows of the table and similar to execute the outer query you need to examine n rows, so in total n + n = 2n rows.

This is the reason you should be very careful using a correlated subquery with large tables e.g. tables with millions of rows because that can take a long time and could potentially block other jobs and queries from accessing the table.

In many cases, you can replace correlated subquery with inner join which would result in better performance. For example, to find all employees whose salary is greater than the average salary of the department you can write the following correlated subquery:

```
SELECT e.id, e.name
FROM Employee e
WHERE salary > (
SELECT AVG(salary)
FROM Employee p
WHERE p.department = e.department)
```

Now, you can convert this correlated subquery to a JOIN based query for better performance as shown below:

```
SELECT e.id, e.name
FROM Employee INNER JOIN
(SELECT department, AVG(salary) AS department_average
FROM Employee
GROUP BY department) AS t ON e.department = t.department
WHERE e.salary > t.department_average;
```

That's all about the **difference between correlated and non-correlated subquery in SQL**. You have learned that correlated subquery is executed for each row returned by an outer query, which makes it very slow, but at the same time gives it the power to compare one row of the table to other rows of the table. That's why sometimes the only solution possible was only by using a correlated subquery.

On the other hand regular or non-correlated subquery return a result which is then used by the outer query. It is only executed one time and not for every row returned by the outer query, hence it is faster than a correlated subquery.

Difference between Self and Equi Join in SQL

The main difference between Self Join and Equi Join is that In Self Join we join one table to itself rather than joining two tables. Both Self Join and Equi Join are types of INNER Join in SQL, but there is a subtle difference between the two. Any INNER Join with equal as join predicate is known as Equi Join. SQL Joins are the fundamental concept of SQL similar to correlated and noncorrelated subqueries or using group by clause and a good understanding of various types of SQL join is a must for any programmer.

By the way, If you have written INNER join using where clause then using a comparison operator as = will be known as an equijoin. Equi joins or Self-join is not a formal JOIN or part of the syntax, instead, they are a just popular way to refer to certain join examples.

One of the best examples of Self Join, I have seen in an SQL query Interview questions is *"How do you find all Employees who are Managers in Employee table"*, which is commonly asked along with another popular question how to find the second highest salary of employee or questions related to joining three tables in one SQL query.

In this SQL tutorial, we will learn to self-join by example while solving this SQL query. Btw, If you are new to SQL and don't understand fundamentals like JOINs or co-related sub-queries then I highly recommend you go through a comprehensive SQL course like**The Complete SQL Bootcamp** by Jose Portilla on Udemy. It's one of the best and also most affordable courses to learn SQL online.

How to remove duplicates from a table?

There are a couple of ways to remove duplicate rows from a table in SQL e.g. you can use temp tables or a window function like row_number() to generate artificial ranking and remove the duplicates. By using a temp table, you can first copy all unique records into a temp table and then delete all data from the original table and then copy unique records again to the original table. This way, **all duplicate rows will be removed**, but with large tables, this solution will require additional space of the same magnitude as the original table. The second approach doesn't require extra space as it removes duplicate rows directly from the table. It uses a ranking function like `row_number()` to assign a row number to each row.

By using **partition by** clause you can reset the row numbers on a particular column. In this approach, all unique rows will have row number = 1 and duplicate rows will have `row_number > 1`, which gives you an easy option to remove those duplicate rows. You can do that by using a **common table expression** (see T-SQL Fundamentals) or without it on Microsoft SQL Server.

No doubt that SQL queries are an integral part of any programming job interview which requires database and SQL knowledge. The queries are also very interesting to check the candidate's logical reasoning ability.

Earlier, I have shared a list of frequently asked SQL queries from interviews and this article is an extension of that. I have shared a lot of good SQL-based problems on that article and users have also shared some excellent problems in the comments, which you should look at.

Btw, this is the follow-up question of another popular SQL interview question, how do you find duplicate records in a table, which we have discussed earlier.

This is an interesting question because many candidates confuse themselves easily.

Some candidate says that they will find duplicate by using group by and printing name which has counted more than 1, but when it comes to deleting this approach doesn't work, because if you delete using this logic both duplicate and unique row will get deleted.

This little bit of extra detail like `row_number` makes this problem challenging for many programmers who don't use SQL on a daily basis. Now, let's see our solution to *delete duplicate rows from a table* in SQL Server.

3 Ways to Remove duplicate values from a table using SQL Query

Before exploring a solution, let's first create the table and populate it with test data to understand both problems and solutions better. I am using a temp table to avoid leaving test data into the database once we are done. Since temp tables are cleaned up once you close the connection to the database, they are best suited for testing.

In our table, I have just one column for simplicity, if you have multiple columns then the definition of duplicate depends on whether all columns should be equal or some key columns e.g. name and city can be the same for two unique persons. In such cases, you need to extend the solution by using those columns on key places e.g. on a distinct clause in the first solution and on the partition by in the second solution.

Anyway, here is our temp table with test data, it is carefully constructed to have duplicates, you can see that C++ is repeated thrice while Java is repeated twice in the table.

```
-- create a temp table for testing
create table #programming (name varchar(10));
-- insert data with duplicate, C++ is repeated 3 times,
while Java 2 times
insert into #programming values ('Java');
insert into #programming values ('C++');
insert into #programming values ('JavaScript');
insert into #programming values ('Python');
insert into #programming values ('C++');
insert into #programming values ('Java');
insert into #programming values ('C++');
-- cleanup
drop table #programming
```

1. How to remove duplicate in SQL using temp table - Example

Yes, this is the most simple but logical way to remove duplicate elements from a table and it will work across databases like MySQL, Oracle, or SQL Server. The idea is to copy unique rows into a temp table. You can find unique rows by using a distinct clause.

Once unique rows are copied, delete everything from the original table and then copy unique rows again. This way, all the duplicate rows have been removed as shown below.

```
-- removing duplicate using copy, delete and copy
select distinct name into #unique from #programming
delete from #programming;
insert into #programming select * from #unique
-- check after
select * from #programming
name
Java
C++
JavaScript
Python
```

You can see the duplicate occurrences of Java and C++ have been removed from the #programming temp table.

2. Delete Duplicates using row_number() and derived table - Example

The `row_number()` is one of several ranking functions provided by SQL Server, It also exists in the Oracle database. You can use this function to provide ranking to rows. You can further use partition to tell SQL server that what would be the window.

This way row number will restart as soon as a different name comes up but for the same name, all rows will get sequential numbers e.g. 1, 2, 3, etc. Now, it's easy to spot the duplicates in the derived table as shown in the following example:

```
select * from (select *, row_number()
OVER ( partition by name order by name) as rn
from #programming) dups
name rn
C++ 1
C++ 2
C++ 3
Java 1
Java 2
JavaScript 1
Python 1
```

Now, you can *remove all the duplicates* which are nothing but rows with `rn > 1`, as done by following SQL query:

```
delete dups
from (select *, row_number()
over ( partition by name order by name) as rn
from #programming)
dups
WHERE rn > 1
(3 row(s) affected)
```

Now, if you check the `#programming` table again there won't be any duplicates.

```
select *from #programming
name
Java
C++
JavaScript
Python
```

252

This is by far the simplest solution and also quite easy to understand but it doesn't come to your mind without practicing. I suggest solving some SQL puzzles from Joe Celko's classic book, **SQL Puzzles, and Answers**, Second Edition to develop your SQL sense. It's a great practice book to learn and master SQL logic.

3. How to remove duplicates using CTE (Common Table Expression)

Example: The CTE stands for common table expression, which is similar to a <u>derived table</u> and used to the temporary result set that is defined within the execution scope of a single SELECT, INSERT, UPDATE, DELETE, or CREATE VIEW statement. Similar to a derived table, CTE is also not stored as an object and lasts only for the duration of the query.

You can rewrite the previous solution using CTE as shown below:

```
;with cte
as (select row_number()
over (partition by name order by(select 0)) rn
from #programming)
delete from cte where rn > 1
```

The logic is exactly similar to the previous example and I am using select 0 because it's arbitrary which rows to preserve in the event of a tie as both contents the same data. If you are new to CTE then I suggest reading <u>T-SQL Fundamentals</u>, one of the best books to learn SQL Server fundamentals.

Here is a nice summary of all three ways to remove duplicates from a table using SQL:

3 Ways to Remove Duplicates from a table in SQL

1. Using temp table

2. Using row_number() window function

3. Using CTE (Common table expression)

That's all about **how to remove duplicate rows from a table in SQL**. As I said, this is one of the frequently asked SQL queries, so be prepared for that when you go for your programming job interview.

I have tested the query in SQL Server 2008 and they work fine and you might need to tweak them a little bit depending upon the database you are going to use like MySQL, Oracle, or PostgreSQL. Feel free to post, if you face any issue while removing duplicates in Oracle, MySQL, or any other database.

How to find all the customers who have never ordered anything?

We have four customers with Id ranging from 1 to 4. Our second table, Orders, contains Id, which is a unique id for order, and `CustomerId`, which is the Id of the Customer who makes that order. If any Customer will place an order, then their Id will exist in the Orders table.

Table: Customers.

```
+----+-------+
| Id | Name  |
+----+-------+
| 1  | Joe   |
| 2  | Henry |
| 3  | Sam   |
| 4  | Max   |
+----+-------+
```

Table: Orders.

```
+-----+------------+
| Id  | CustomerId |
+-----+------------+
|  1  |  3  |
|  2  |  1  |
+-----+------------+
```

Using the above tables as an example, return the following:

```
+------------+
| Customers  |
+------------+
| Henry |
| Max   |
+------------+
```

How to Find Customers Who Never Order using EXISTS in SQL

One of the most common solutions to this problem is by using the SQL JOIN clause. You can use the <u>LEFT OUTER JOIN</u> to solve this problem, as shown below:

```
SELECT C.Name FROM Customers C
LEFT JOIN Orders O ON  C.Id = O.CustomerId
WHERE O.CustomerId is NULL
```

When you join two tables in SQL using a <u>LEFT OUTER JOIN</u>, then a big table will be created with NULL values in the column which don't exist in another table.

For example, the big table will have four columns C.Id, C.Name, O.Id, and O.CustomerId, for Customers who have never ordered anything, the O.CustomerId will be <u>NULL</u>.

Many programmers make the mistake of using != in the JOIN condition to solve this problem, with the assumption that if = returns matching rows, then != will return those ids which are not present in another table. So beware of that..

Anyway, this problem is actually an excellent example of **how and when to use EXISTS clause:**

```
SELECT C.Name FROM Customers C
WHERE NOT EXISTS (SELECT1FROM Orders O WHERE C.Id =
O.CustomerId)
```

This is a <u>correlated subquery</u>, where the inner query will execute for each row of the outer query, and only those customers will be returned who have not ordered anything.

Btw, the most simple solution is by using the NOT IN Clause.

```
SELECT A.Name FROM Customers A
WHERE A.Id NOT IN (SELECT B.CustomerId FROMs Orders B)
And, here is a nice screenshot to remember how and when
to use the EXISTS clause in SQL query:
```

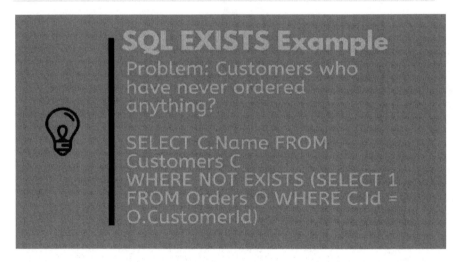

That's all about **how to use the EXISTS clause in SQL** to find all customers who have never ordered. If you like to improve your SQL query skills, then you can also problems given in Joe Celko's classical book SQL Puzzles and Answers, the 2nd Edition. One of the best books with lots of challenging questions to test your SQL skill, and if you need some online courses to learn SQL in-depth or fill the gaps in your SQL knowledge, the following courses are a good place to start with.

How to find Duplicate emails in a table?

You need to write a SQL query to find all duplicate emails in a table named Person. This is a popular SQL Query interview question as well as a Leetcode problem. You can see that email a@b.com is a duplicate email as it appears twice in the table.

Given below table, write an SQL query to find all duplicate values (Emails)

```
+----+----------+
| Id | Email    |
+----+----------+
| 1  | a@b.com  |
| 2  | c@d.com  |
| 3  | a@b.com  |
+----+----------+
```

For example, your query should return the following for the above table:

```
+----------+
| Email    |
+----------+
| a@b.com  |
+----------+
```

Note: All emails are in lowercase.

Here are three ways to solve this problem in SQL query, first by using group by clause, second by using self-join, and then third by using subquery with exists clause.

While I agree that this problem can be solved in a different way, but it is also a perfect example of how you can use the **SQL GROUP BY and HAVING clause**.

But, if you are new to the SQL world, it's better to start with a comprehensive SQL course like **The Complete SQL Bootcamp course** by Jose Portilla on Udemy.

That will help you to learn SQL better and quicker, and these kinds of articles will also make more sense once you have some SQL knowledge under your belt.

```
SELECT FirstName
    ,DuplicateCount = COUNT(1)
FROM SalesLT.Customer
GROUP BY FirstName
HAVING COUNT(1) > 1    -- more than one value
ORDER BY COUNT(1) DESC -- sort by most duplicates|
```

	FirstName	DuplicateCount
1	Robert	12
2	John	10
3	Michael	8
4	Scott	6
5	James	6
6	David	6
7	Linda	5
8	Mary	5
9	Matthew	4

1. Finding Duplicate elements By using GROUP BY

The simplest solution to this problem is by using the GROUP BY and HAVING Clause. Use GROUP BY to group the result set on email, this will bring all duplicate emails in one group, now if the count for a particular email is greater than 1 it means it is a duplicate email. Here is the SQL query to find duplicate emails:

Write your MySQL query statement below

```
SELECT Email FROM Person
GROUP BY Email
HAVINGCOUNT(Email) >1
```

This is also my accepted answer on LeetCode. You can see by using the count function you can count a number of elements in the group and if your group contains more than 1 row then it's a duplicate value that you want to print.

2. Finding Duplicate values in a column by using Self Join

By the way, there are a couple of more ways to solve this problem, one is by using Self Join. If you remember, In Self Join we join two instances of the same table to compare one record to another. Now if an email from one record in the first instance of the table is equal to the email of another record in the second table it means the email is duplicate. Here is the SQL query using Self Join

Write your MySQL query statement below

```
SELECT DISTINCT a.Email FROM Person a
JOIN   Person b ON a.Email = b. Email
WHERE a.Id != b.Id
```

Remember to use the keyword distinct here because it will print the duplicate email as many times it appears in the table. This is also an accepted solution in Leetcode.

3. Finding duplicate emails By using Sub-query with EXISTS:

You can even solve this problem using a correlated subquery. In a correlated subquery, the inner query is executed for each record in the outer query. So one email is compared to the rest of the email in the same table using a correlated subquery and EXISTS clause in SQL as shown below.

Here is the solution query :

```
SELECT DISTINCT p1.Email
FROM Person p1
WHERE EXISTS(
SELECT*
FROM Person p2
WHERE p2.Email = p1.Email
AND p2.Id != p1.Id
)
```

CHAPTER 14

Conclusion

Software Engineering and Technical Interview is not easy as you can see there are a lot of topics to master and a lot of concepts to cover. Given the importance of SQL in Software Development and Data Science, it becomes extremely important for any developer or Data Scientist to have a strong knowledge of Database concepts and SQL.

You can use this book in many ways, for example, you can use it to revise frequently asked SQL questions and concepts before you for any telephonic or face-to-face Software Engineering and Data Science interview as well as to get an idea of essential concepts.

The book covers a lot of ground, including the basics of SQL queries and database design, as well as more advanced topics like indexes, stored procedures, triggers, and normalization. Additionally, the book provides numerous real-world SQL interview questions, giving readers ample opportunities to practice and refine their skills.

Whether you are a beginner or an experienced SQL developer or Data Scientist, this book has something to offer. The author has taken great care to explain complex concepts in a simple and easy-to-understand manner, making it accessible to all levels of learners.

Overall, **Grokking the SQL Interview is a must-read for anyone looking to prepare for a SQL interview**. The book provides valuable insights into the most commonly asked SQL interview questions and offers practical advice on how to approach them.

So, if you are preparing for an SQL interview or looking to brush up on your SQL skills, this book is definitely worth a read.

Once again, thanks for reading this book and I wish it fulfills your expectations. Don't forget to leave ratings and give feedback as they help us to create more such books and make them even better.

All the best for your Software Engineering and Data Science interview.

Made in the USA
Las Vegas, NV
16 January 2024

84483681R00157